Family Circles

LONGMAN IMPRINT BOOKS

Family Circles

Five plays for radio
by

Gilly Fraser
David Luck
Wally K. Daly
Chris Curry
Peter Whalley

selected and edited by
Alfred Bradley and **Alison Leake**

Longman

LONGMAN GROUP LIMITED
Longman House
Burnt Mill, Harlow, Essex CM20 2JE, England
and Associated Companies throughout the World

First published by arrangement with the British Broadcasting Corporation 1984
ISBN 0 582 22111 0

Set in 10/11pt Baskerville Linotron 202

Printed in Hong Kong by
Commonwealth Printing Press Ltd

We are grateful to London Weekend Television for permission to reproduce photographs.

Cover by Jane Taylor

Contents

Family Circles

An introductory note

Radio Drama has a strong claim to be called the National Theatre of the Air. More than 500 plays are broadcast by the BBC each year and although many of them are adaptations of stage plays or novels a good proportion are specially written with radio in mind.

It is surprising that few of the scripts find their way into print especially as the economy of radio gives it a great advantage over other forms of drama production. The ease with which radio plays may be brought to life without the need for elaborate technical resources makes them particularly useful in the classroom.

The five plays included in this volume have been chosen to reflect the joys and problems of family life. *It's A Wise Child* tells the story of an adopted boy who goes in search of the mother who deserted him at birth; *Little Weed's Big Day* is an account of the family stresses which play a large part in a teenager's first day at work; *A Quick Visit Home* is a study of the differences that arise between two sisters who have to decide how best to look after their recently widowed mother; *Home Truths* shows us how members of a family begin to question their beliefs and relationships when a young man brings his girlfriend home for the first time; and *Voice Downstairs, Ears Upstairs* is a comedy about the problems which arise as a father tries to look after his handicapped son during his wife's stay in hospital.

The texts are almost identical with the original radio scripts, but the studio directions have been simplified so that they can be read in the classroom. At the same time the sound effects are easily picked out if you decide to go a step further and record a full-scale radio production. Despite the complex and expensive equipment used in professional broadcasting studios, a great deal can be achieved using a school tape recorder, and with patience and ingenuity it should be possible to create all of the effects in the plays without difficulty. Detailed suggestions for the setting up of a simple studio and notes on radio production are given in Producing Radio Plays in Schools at the end of the book.

cord a full-scale radio production. Despite the complex and expensive equipment used in professional broadcasting studios, a great deal can be achieved using a school tape recorder, and with patience and ingenuity it should be possible to create all of the effects in the plays without difficulty. Detailed suggestions for the setting up of a simple studio and notes on radio production are given in *Producing Radio Plays in Schools* at the end of the book.

A Quick Visit Home

Gilly Fraser

The Cast

Pat

Jim

Lynne

Mother

Ada

A Quick Visit Home

1 The chapel of a crematorium

As the canned organ music ends Pat turns to her husband.

PAT Is that it then?

JIM I reckon.

PAT Ten minutes from that lad, who calls himself a vicar, and the coffin slides away?

JIM It's what your Dad wanted – cremation.

PAT What a bloody daft thing to say.

JIM Pat! You're in chapel!

PAT Well it is. Anyroad, how do you know what he wanted?

Aunt Ada can be heard crying noisily in the background.

There goes me Aunty Ada turning on the waterworks again.

LYNNE Should we go now do you think?

PAT How the hell should I know?

LYNNE Thanks very much!

JIM I should think so, Lynne.

PAT Well I'm not stopping here all morning.

General shuffle as the congregation rises.

JIM You and Lynne and your Mam are chief mourners – I suppose you should go first.

LYNNE Nobody cares about that nowadays.

JIM I think we should go now, Mother.

MOTHER I know what to do, thank you very much. I was going to funerals before you were born.

ADA (*Sobbing*) Oh Alice.

MOTHER Pull yourself together, Ada. Lynne! Take your Aunty outside.

LYNNE Come on, Aunty.

JIM Take my arm, Mother.

MOTHER I'm not a cripple yet. I'll manage on my own.

Mother, Ada and Lynne walk up the aisle.

PAT They're not doing that to me when I go.

JIM Don't be morbid, love.

PAT I'll leave my body to the hospital. I can do without all this rigmarole. Just look. A right pair, they are.

JIM What?

PAT Our Lynne and Aunt Ada, sobbing away there. You wouldn't think they never came near when he was ill, would you?

JIM Now then. You know what we said.

PAT All right. I heard. It just makes me sick, that's all.

2 The crematorium garden

LYNNE Me Mam and Ada are talking to the vicar or whatever he was.

PAT I thought it were policemen that were supposed to look young. He looked about fourteen.

JIM I expect he were the curate.

PAT That's just like me dad to get second best.

LYNNE It seemed so awful in that funny little chapel with no proper service or anything.

PAT Oh get off! When was the last time you were in church unless it was a posh wedding with your smart London friends?

LYNNE What's that got to do with it? I'd rather he'd had nothing than that gabbled farce.

PAT What *you'd* 'rather' is neither here nor there.

JIM You've got to admit you were just saying more or less the same.

PAT Where's these cars then? They should be here now.

JIM They'll be along in a minute.

LYNNE I'll go and give my Aunty a hand down the steps. (*She goes.*)

PAT She should feel the cold with a couple of hundred quids worth of fur coat on her back.

JIM You can be a right bitch at times. I expect she earned the money to pay for it.

PAT She always did well for herself, that one.

MOTHER (*approaching*) What's happened to the cars? They should be here waiting, there's the tea to get on.

PAT There's only the tea to make. I've laid out everything else.

MOTHER They'll be curling at the edges. If there's one thing I can't abide it's curled sandwiches.

PAT I've already told you I've covered them with polythene.

MOTHER It's not the same... you'd better go and have a word with Mr Slocombe or we'll be here all day.

JIM I'll go. Here's Aunt Ada with Lynne.

LYNNE There's a bench if you want to sit down, Aunty.

ADA I'm all right for the minute, Lynne... It weren't a bad funeral, Alice.

MOTHER It shouldn't have been. I've been paying insurance long enough.

ADA I'm not so sure as I like this cremating. I like a nice headstone meself. We had a beauty for Ernest.

MOTHER It's more hygienic... and quick. You can catch your death standing round graves.

ADA I don't know how you do it. I really don't. I were only saying to our John this morning, *you'll* not have to come back when your time comes.

MOTHER That's as may be.

ADA If only you'd let us know sooner we'd have been round like a shot... if we could have left the shop. It's our busy time.

PAT (*icy*) We're lucky to have you here today.

ADA It took a lot of working out, I don't mind telling you. As it is your Uncle John will have to do the Sharpes' order... Aye dear – when I think – he were a good brother to me.

MOTHER There's Jim with the cars now. You go with Mrs Armitage, Lynne, and your Aunty and I'll go in front with Pat.

She goes taking Pat with her.

ADA She allus was a strong woman, your mother. Mind you, she's not what you could call sensitive... she's never suffered with her nerves like I have. You look right well, Lynne. Your Mam says you've been writing them telly commercials. How did you get on to that then? The last I heard you were a secretary.

LYNNE I got promoted.

ADA Fancy.

LYNNE I think we'd better...

ADA Our Kevin would have been here, you know, but for his exams...he's taking his finals soon. He's a good lad to me. He's not got bigheaded, I'll give him that. Telly commercials, eh? Our Kev's girlfriend does those. She's a model, you know, in Manchester. Sharon Clegg. I expect you'll know of her.

LYNNE I don't think so.

ADA I'm surprised. She's right well known. Lovely girl, they're thinking of getting engaged at Whit.

LYNNE That's nice.

ADA Have you got any plans...in that direction?

LYNNE No. (*Moving off*) We'd better get in the car, they're waiting.

ADA Writing telly commercials! I can't get over it. After all that education.

3 The kitchen (later that night)

PAT That's the last. I thought they'd never go.

LYNNE I'd no idea the front room could hold so many people. Come to think of it, that's only the third time I've seen her use the front room, except for Christmas.

PAT My wedding and that time the police came to tell her about Uncle George.

LYNNE I remember her playing Hamlet when I sneaked in there with Rita Fieldhouse...you bet me a penny I wouldn't have the cheek.

PAT (*about to reply but stops herself and breaks the intimacy*) I don't remember... Aunt Ada was really getting on my wick, all that stuff about being too busy with 'the business' when Mam needed help. 'Business', you'd think they were running ICI instead of a tuppenny ha'penny sweetshop.

JIM You can't shut up shop just like that, you know.

PAT They could have done more than they did...you're putting those knives in the wrong drawer, Lynne. Here I'll take them.

LYNNE Where are the tea towels?

PAT Under your nose – where they always were.

LYNNE How's she taking it?

PAT Have you ever known her show her feelings?

LYNNE Was it . . . very bad?

PAT Yes. If you want a straight answer.

LYNNE I'd no idea . . .

PAT There's no point in going over it all now. No doubt she'll tell you about it.

LYNNE But . . . oh never mind.

PAT (*after a pause*) That's a nice coat you had on. I bet that cost a bob or two. You must be earning a fair whack then, since you got promoted . . . you can't dress like that on peanuts.

LYNNE I'm doing okay.

PAT Mind you, I think they're a load of rubbish myself.

LYNNE What?

PAT Commercials.

LYNNE Thanks.

PAT You always were a jammy devil . . . what a job, eh?

LYNNE What's that supposed to mean?

PAT Come on. You don't tell me it takes you all day to write one of them things.

LYNNE You want to try it some time.

PAT I'll tell you what work is . . . it's running a house and bringing up three kids . . . you'll find out when you get married.

LYNNE No doubt.

PAT You're not thinking of settling then? You've no one in mind?

LYNNE No.

PAT I just wondered.

JIM Any chance of a cup of tea?

PAT You know where the pot is.

JIM I'll put the kettle on.

PAT Anyroad, it'll be a help to me Mam to see a bit of you now you are here. She talks of nowt else.

JIM I wouldn't go as far as that.

LYNNE But I can't stay . . . you didn't think I was staying did you?

PAT I don't believe it!

LYNNE Hell Pat . . . I've got to work. You don't understand.

PAT My god! You don't change much, do you? That's

typical of you. Bloody typical! I don't know how you can stand there and have the brassneck!

LYNNE Look, I didn't know there was all this trouble at home, did I? If I had I could have done something. As it is . . .

PAT Whose fault was that?

JIM Steady on, Pat. Be fair . . . you know what your Mam's like.

PAT She should make it her business to know. If she came home a bit more often she'd know what was going on.

LYNNE There was nothing to stop you letting me know, was there?

PAT I had enough to do without worrying about you.

LYNNE It wouldn't have taken you five minutes to ring me and at least warn me he was ill. You didn't want me to know!

PAT I've never heard anything so daft! What sort of stupid remark is that? I'd got too much on my mind. The world doesn't revolve around you, you know.

JIM The kettle's boiling . . . Come on now, a cup of tea will do us all good.

PAT I don't see you being much help now. You haven't even got the decency to stay until we get things settled.

LYNNE I've told you I have to work. I've no choice; you can't take time off in the middle of a big campaign.

JIM That's true.

PAT What do you know about it?

JIM I know what it's like in our office.

PAT To hell with your office. Doesn't anybody die in advertising then?

JIM Steady on.

PAT Whose side are you on?

JIM It's not a question of . . .

PAT If *I* could manage with all I've got on my plate . . .

LYNNE You don't know what you're talking about. You haven't the faintest idea what it's like.

PAT So you keep telling me. Right – we'll talk about things now.

LYNNE What 'things'?

PAT You know very well.

JIM I don't think this is the time.

LYNNE I'd very much like to know just what's bugging you – because I'm damn sure something is.

PAT Don't you patronise me. You come waltzing down here in your smart gear thinking you're doing us all a favour just by your illustrious presence . . .

JIM Pat! We're not going to get anywhere with you two like cat and dog. Your mother'll be down any minute – you don't want her to hear, do you?

LYNNE Hear what? Will you please tell me what's the matter?

JIM I'll pour out the tea and then we can talk about this calmly and rationally.

PAT I don't want any.

JIM (*pouring the tea*) Well I do. Do you take sugar, Lynne?

LYNNE No thanks.

JIM Right. I hope it's not too strong.

PAT I would have thought with all your education you would have seen it staring you straight in the face . . . it's me Mam we're on about.

LYNNE What about her?

JIM You've admitted you're doing all right – earning a fair amount down there . . .

PAT It's not that we don't want her. I'll not have you think that.

JIM She'll need some persuading though.

LYNNE What are you talking about?

PAT We're thinking of the future. A home for her.

LYNNE But she's got a home.

PAT Don't you think of anyone but yourself? This place is too much for her. I know. I've seen.

LYNNE (*anxious*) She's not ill?

PAT Suppose she's taken bad, all alone here. Who's to know? There isn't a neighbour she hasn't had words with. We're settled in Leeds now, Jim's doing well and the kiddies are at good schools . . . we're not moving back here, I'll tell you that for nothing.

LYNNE Who said you should? I don't understand . . .

A door shuts upstairs.

JIM Hush. She's coming down.

The kitchen door opens.

MOTHER They're hard on. They're devils, those bairns. I thought I'd never get them off.

PAT You let them play you up.

MOTHER Our Jackie's got more off than a load of monkeys... he's a right lad.

PAT You shouldn't let them tire you like that. Especially today.

MOTHER It's a pleasure to see to them. I don't see nearly enough of them. I've given the baby a dummy... I had it put by in the drawer.

PAT Oh Mam! You know I don't like it.

MOTHER I've looked after more bairns than you've had hot dinners... it's a bit of comfort for her.

PAT I've told you before, Mam, it'll spoil her mouth.

MOTHER It never spoiled yours. Or our Lynne's for that matter. I've sorted out your dad's stuff – it can go to the Chapel Jumble... there's many would be glad of it.

LYNNE You shouldn't have done that on your own. If you'd given a shout I'd have helped you.

MOTHER Your Aunt Ada was after your dad's watch – I saw her looking. I've put it on one side for our Jackie. He can have it when he's old enough to appreciate it.

PAT Thanks. He always used to like his Grandad's watch.

LYNNE So did we when we were little. Do you remember how we used to fight to get on his knee to play with it and he used to smack us both for rowing... and then made puppets out of his hankie to make us laugh.

MOTHER (*breaking the mood*) Who's put these knives in water? The handles'll get ruined.

LYNNE I'm sorry.

MOTHER I might have known. You always were the careless one.

PAT I wish you'd sit down, Mam. You've been on your feet all day.

JIM Come on, Mother. You're not as young as you were! Take this chair.

MOTHER I'll sit down when I'm ready... It'd do you good to be on your feet a bit more. You're getting fat.

PAT He has to sit down all day in his job. I keep telling him to join the squash club or go to Weight Watchers or summat... Mam! There's no need to put those away yet. Will you sit down and get your tea? We want to talk to you.

MOTHER I thought you *were* doing.

JIM We didn't mean to bring it up quite so soon...

PAT But as it seems our Lynne's off again as usual, we've got to get things settled now.

LYNNE There's no need to put it like that... I'm sorry, love. I've got to go straight back to London, tomorrow. I can't get out of it.

MOTHER To do with your work is it?

LYNNE It's the first job I've had to handle on my own.

MOTHER I'm glad you're getting your chance.

LYNNE I don't *make* the film you know – I only write the script – some of it – sometimes.

MOTHER I like to see what you're doing. What's it for?

LYNNE Starspray hair lacquer.

PAT Bloody hell! Is that all they taught you at the university? You want to find out what real work is.

LYNNE I'd like to see you face up to a day at the pressure I work under.

PAT Pressure? Writing daft rhymes for the telly? 'Starspray Hair Lacquer makes you bald'... get on!

MOTHER We'll have no more of that. It's wonderful how our Lynne's got on.

PAT Oh yeah!

MOTHER Your job's your job, and you've got to put your back into it if you want owt out of life.

PAT Write two silly rhymes a day instead of one.

JIM We shan't get anywhere at this rate. We've got to talk.

MOTHER Nobody's stopping you.

JIM About the future... Pat and I thought... this house is too big and your chest's been bad...

PAT I don't see how you can go living here on your own.

MOTHER I beg your pardon.

PAT You know damn well it's too much for you. We're in Leeds and our Lynne's in London. There's nothing else for it – we'll just have to come to some arrangement – between us.

LYNNE Just what did you have in mind?

PAT If you'd any decency you'd have offered. You've got a flat of your own and money, and what's more important, no kids to worry about.

LYNNE It's one room with a kitchen and shower!

PAT So what? You can get a bigger one, all the money you

earn. This house is damp and cold and her chest won't stand another winter in it.

JIM You'd get a good price for the house. It's really coming up, this area. I can arrange it for you through the firm, it's no trouble.

LYNNE Is that right about your chest? Have you been to the doctor's?

MOTHER There's nowt up with me.

PAT Listen to her! You want to hear her coughing sometimes.

MOTHER When you've quite finished talking about me as if I were deaf or daft. I'll let you know when I'm losing my faculties... when I want your Jim to sell my house over my head I'll let him know.

JIM I was only trying...

MOTHER I've no intentions of leaving this house and if I had I wouldn't burden Lynne. She's got her own life to lead.

PAT What do you think I do all day? Paint my toenails? I'm up to here with being Old Muggins Pat, endlessly lumbered with all the dirty work no one else wants to do.

MOTHER Give over, you daft bitch. I've never...

PAT She was the one who had the elocution lessons so she could learn to talk posh...

LYNNE But I hated them!

PAT I got stuck with the washing up because madame here was doing her homework and nothing had to interfere with that!

LYNNE Hasn't it ever occurred to you that I might have minded being stuck in doing homework while you went out whenever you wanted to? I'll never forget that time Dad took you to the fair and I had to stay behind doing maths. I cried myself silly over that.

PAT I remember when you were talking your 'A' levels... it was the same year I got married. There was no doubt in my mind which came first with me Mam – I couldn't even have a June wedding because of your stupid exams!

LYNNE That was hardly my fault.

MOTHER I'll not listen to that rubbish, Pat. You had every

chance . . . the same as our Lynne. You couldn't leave school fast enough.

PAT Too right. I wanted to get on with living. She never knew what day it was. She always had her head in some stupid book, swotting.

MOTHER You couldn't be bothered. She used her brains.

PAT She has and all. To get as far away from here as possible. She's far too grand for the likes of us. Well, I'll tell you something. I'm proud of my home and my kids. They're more than she's managed for all her scholarships.

LYNNE For God's sake, Pat!

PAT All she ever talks about is you. "Our Lynne's passed her exams", "Our Lynne's going to the university", "Our Lynne's got a good job in London". She raised a cheer every time you went to the lav. And what does she get in return? I'll tell you what. A letter every six months and a cheque birthdays and Christmas. Ask her to take her share, to pay back what's due – oh no! That's another matter.

MOTHER Shut your mouth! We'll have no more of that talk in this house. You ought to be ashamed squabbling like that with your Dad only just put to rest. You're no better than you were as kids. And we'll have no more about me leaving this house – I don't know how you can have the gall to suggest such a thing. Anyone would think I was an old woman. I'm going up now – but I'll tell you this, Pat, if you don't think I value you and the children you're even stupider than I thought.

She goes out closing the door behind her.

LYNNE I never knew you felt like that.

PAT Well now you know, don't you?

4 A bedroom

An alarm clock ticks in the background.

JIM How long are you going to be? You've been fiddling about there for ages.

PAT Just a minute.

JIM Come to bed for God's sake. I've had enough for one night.

PAT You've had enough! Do you expect me to lie down and go to sleep after all that?

JIM Oh give it a rest, will you? If you'd kept your temper we might have got somewhere.

PAT Our Lynne always rubs me up the wrong way. She'd never even given it thought. All she thinks about is that bloody job of hers.

JIM Give her a chance. It wasn't her fault she knew nowt about your dad being ill. Your Mam didn't even tell *you* until the last couple of weeks.

PAT She could have given thought to what was going to happen to Mam. I suppose she expects me to do it just like always.

JIM She didn't seem all that unreasonable to me. If we could have talked about it calmly and logically...

PAT You and your logic! All talk and no action!

JIM What the bloody hell do you expect me to do? Tie your mother up and ship her down to London in a packing case?

PAT You fancy her don't you?

JIM Who? Your Mam?

PAT Our Lynne! I saw you looking. Well it's all clothes and make up. She wasn't much when she was a kid.

JIM For God's sake!

PAT I could look better than that on her money.

JIM Have I ever stopped you buying clothes?

PAT On what you earn? Don't make me laugh! I wouldn't care if you had a bit of ambition, but no – plod on in the same old way – don't take any chances, that's you.

JIM What are you starting on me for?

PAT You've been stuck in that same job... old man Ferris is never going to take you on as a partner... not with three sons. I wouldn't care but she doesn't know what to do with it when she's got it! That dress was right vulgar...

JIM If you're so keen on bloody money why don't you go out and earn some for yourself?

PAT Have you gone out of your mind? I've got a house and three kids to look after – or have you forgotten?

JIM Other women manage it.

PAT I'll tell you how they manage it – by lumbering women like me. Who runs the PTA jumble sale and lets the gas man in for half the street? I do. Our house is always full of other folks' kids with nowhere to go because their mums are out at work, sitting on their bottoms typing while their kids run wild in the streets.

JIM Get on. You martyr yourself because you enjoy it. Just like your Mam. Anyroad, your Mam would mind the kids if she came to Leeds. It would solve this hoo ha anyway.

PAT What did you say?

JIM It'd be a solution. She needn't live with us – we could get her a flat nearby. She could mind the baby and the other two could go there after school. You'd do right well, they're paying a fortune for shorthand typists nowadays. I don't know why we didn't think of it before.

PAT Stop it! How can you talk like that? I won't have her taking over my life, I won't. They're my kids and I'll bring them up my way with no interference from her. I won't have her there – not at any price, do you hear? I won't!

5 Lynne's bedroom

Mother taps on the door and comes in.

MOTHER I thought you might like some cocoa, love.

LYNNE You shouldn't have been making cocoa for me. You ought to be resting.

MOTHER I'm not tired. When I am I'll rest. Anybody'd think I was senile. Mind you don't spill it down that fancy nightie – it'll take some washing and ironing with all those frills, but you never were one for the practical, were you?

LYNNE You've kept my room just as it was. All my old books and everything.

MOTHER I see no reason to change owt.

LYNNE You've got to, you know. Sooner or later. We all

have. I grew up, Mam. Why do you want to keep a little girl's room?

MOTHER You'll be needing an extra blanket.

LYNNE Why didn't you tell me? About Dad.

MOTHER There was no call for you to see such things. I wish you'd learn to hang up your clothes.

LYNNE That's no answer.

MOTHER There was nowt you could have done. What was the point of interrupting your work and coming dashing up here? It wouldn't have altered owt.

LYNNE He was my father. He must have asked to see me.

MOTHER He didn't know how ill he was.

LYNNE You knew. You wrote and told me he had a touch of bronchitis – how could you lie to me like that?

MOTHER He wouldn't have wanted you worried.

LYNNE Is that what he wanted, or what you wanted? (*Pause*) Will you stop fussing round this room and talk to me! My Dad was dying and I didn't even know. How do you think I feel?

MOTHER You think too much about what you feel.

LYNNE Pat knew. You could let her share it with you. Why not me?

MOTHER Do you want me to press your frock for the morning?

LYNNE No! Why won't you talk to me? Why won't you let me near? When I was a kid there wasn't a thing I wanted you didn't find a way of getting for me. A bike – a hockey stick, whatever – and I was grateful. I did as I was told. I worked and worked, passed my exams, went to college – did all those things to please you. But you never let me near. You didn't then and you don't now!

MOTHER I've always been right proud of you.

LYNNE When I used to come home from university the first thing you used to say to me was "When are you going back?" You didn't like it if I brought friends home but it was all right if I went to stay with them. You always shut me out.

MOTHER You're talking daft now.

LYNNE Am I? It was the same with my Dad. Every time he tried to get close to you, you pushed him away in one way or another.

MOTHER Don't talk about things you know nowt about!

LYNNE (*pause*) I'm sorry. I shouldn't have said that. Not now. Look mam... I know I haven't written or come home as much as I should... Oh, I don't know... you get so cut off... hell, I earn my living writing and I can't even compose a letter home to my own family. It's all so different down there... I don't know what to say.

MOTHER I'm not complaining.

LYNNE You never did. Pat's right – I've grown away. We haven't any common ground any more and that's wrong. It must be.

MOTHER You don't want to take any notice of our Pat. She allus was on the spiteful side, even as a kid. You're overtired, that's what's the matter with you. Get yourself off to sleep, you've a train to catch in the morning. I'll bring you your breakfast up early.

LYNNE Stop waiting on me, Mam. I'll get my own breakfast. You're the one who could do with the rest.

MOTHER We'll see. It'll all feel different in the morning.

LYNNE Mam...

MOTHER We'll say no more. Goodnight.

LYNNE Goodnight.

6 The kitchen

Lynne is humming as she prepares breakfast.

PAT (*approaching*) You're up early.

LYNNE So are you. Where does she keep the tea?

PAT Top shelf. She likes it strong.

LYNNE I know.

The kettle boils.

Are the kids still asleep?

PAT The baby is. The others are getting dressed.

LYNNE Shall I pour you a cup?

PAT If you like.

Lynne pours the tea.

LYNNE They're nice kids.

PAT I've seen worse.

LYNNE There's some sweets for them in my bag.

PAT I don't allow them to eat sweets.

LYNNE There's no point in taking it out on the kids just because we don't get on.

PAT That's got nothing to do with it.

LYNNE We're sisters, Pat. We shouldn't be like this with each other.

PAT Why this sudden interest in the family?

LYNNE I don't dislike you. Why should I?

PAT It's immaterial to me what you think. Will you mind out of the way? I can't get at the breadboard.

LYNNE If you want to know, I admire you.

PAT You what?

LYNNE You always knew what you wanted and you did it – in spite of Mother.

PAT You think that? You really think that?

LYNNE All along the line. That's something.

PAT You must think I'm really stupid.

LYNNE What?

PAT To fall for patronising rubbish like that. Good grief! You want to make it up with me so that you can go back to London with an easy conscience – well I'm not that daft.

LYNNE Why do you take everything I say the wrong way?

PAT Because I've had cause. You always knew how to twist things to suit yourself. My God, how she pinned her hopes on you. And you can't wait to get on the first train back to London.

LYNNE I'm not going back to London.

PAT What did you say?

LYNNE You heard me the first time.

PAT But you said last night you had to be back. What about your job?

LYNNE That's my problem.

PAT I don't understand.

LYNNE I'm not sure I do either. I just know I'm not going back.

PAT When did you decide all this?

LYNNE Last night.

PAT How long are you staying for?

LYNNE I don't know. Maybe for good.

PAT I'll not have you thinking I'm not doing my share. We'll have to talk about that.

MOTHER (*in the distance*) Get those teeth cleaned, you young monkeys, or I'll be after you!

LYNNE I'll need to talk to her. Can you keep the kids out of the way?

MOTHER (*approaching*) I thought I told you to stop in bed. You've a long journey in front of you. What time's the train? You'd best be there early if you want a seat.

LYNNE I'm not going.

MOTHER Have you gone mental?

LYNNE No.

PAT You'll have to let them know.

LYNNE I'll give them a ring from the call box. I expect they'll send my cards but that's okay. It'll save me working notice.

MOTHER You're not giving up your job!

LYNNE I did a lot of thinking last night, and I'm stopping here until I get things sorted out. I'll have to go back to sell the flat lease but that shouldn't take too long. With that money we can get this place converted or we can let Jim sell the house and buy a bigger one. Big enough for you to have a flat in it – so we're not on top of one another. I'll have to get out of advertising but that's all right. I've got a degree – I can always teach.

PAT She can come to us for holidays and that. I don't want you to think I don't know what's what.

Sounds of children shouting upstairs.

(*calling*) Will you be quiet up there! Jackie? Do you hear?

The baby begins to cry.

Oh heck, that's the baby. I'd better go up. It was nice of you to bring them the sweets, Lynne – I'll let them have a few after their breakfast. (*She goes.*)

LYNNE I'll have my tea and then I'll go down to the corner and ring the office. We'll have to get a phone installed. I want to come home, Mam. I really do. It's real up here. I realise that now.

MOTHER Don't talk so bloody daft.

LYNNE And there's your health – you need looking after.

MOTHER What's wrong with me is old age. There's nowt you can do to stop it.

LYNNE I could help if you'd let me. I learned a few things about myself last night...

MOTHER By all accounts you've learnt nowt. I've never asked owt of you and I'm not starting now.

LYNNE I've had enough, Mam. Of the job, London, all of it. I mean it. I want to come home.

MOTHER Your home's in London.

LYNNE That tiny rathole I live in isn't home. I spend more time at work.

MOTHER So you should if you want to get on.

LYNNE You won't see, will you? Do you know why I work so late? Because I'd lose the job if I didn't. All that stuff you think of me – "Our Lynne, brilliant career girl" – it just isn't true. I finally got my chance as a copywriter and all I've proved to myself is that I'm no bloody good. I can hold my own – just – but it's not good enough. I can't take any more competition. You pushed me up the ladder, Mam, but you never told me I mightn't like the view from the top... What was it all for?

MOTHER You can stand there and ask me that.

LYNNE What have I got? Nothing. Except money.

MOTHER You wouldn't say that if you'd had to do without it.

LYNNE That doesn't answer the question.

MOTHER You've got your independence. You can do what you like, when you like, with nobody to tell you different.

LYNNE I want to do what somebody else likes...oh you don't know what I'm talking about.

MOTHER I do an' all. Have you any idea what it's like to live with a chap with no ambition? Your Dad was a good man – but he never saw further than next week's wages. He had a steady job and he stuck in it for forty years. And what did he get at the end of it? A bloody clock! I married late in life and I rued every day of it except for you kids.

LYNNE Mam!

MOTHER You wanted some plain speaking, well you can have it. I worked and saved so that you could have a life that's a bit more than endless scrimping and making do. You had brains and I made damn sure you used them.

LYNNE You never thought to ask me if it's what I wanted.

MOTHER You don't know what you want. You've got all I ever imagined for you and just because you're having a bit of trouble you come running back to me like a frightened rabbit.

LYNNE Didn't you ever think it might have been your imagination that was at fault?

MOTHER Are you having trouble with some chap, is that it? He'll not be worth it. There's not many that are.

LYNNE All right, I'll tell you something now. He was worth it. His name was David and we were living together. He left me. And do you know why? Because I was earning twice as much as he was and he couldn't stand it.

MOTHER That only goes to prove my point.

LYNNE Does it? He was a teacher. He got a job in Hull in an approved school. He wanted me to marry him and go up there. I said no because I was angling for another stupid promotion. I should have married him. I should have shared his life!

MOTHER If you think you can live your life through a man I've been wasting my time all these years. You'll get married in time if that's what you want, but when you do it'll be on your own terms. That's worth waiting for.

LYNNE What's wrong with me living up here with you? That at least would have some meaning.

MOTHER What meaning is there in a young woman wasting her life for an old one? I can't abide waste. What is there for you up here?

LYNNE I've told you. I could teach.

MOTHER If you'd wanted to be a teacher, you'd have been one. There's enough of them doing it 'cos they can't think of owt else. You're used to earning good money. Once you've had it you can't do without it.

LYNNE I'd manage.

MOTHER You wouldn't know where to start. I managed on your Dad's wages because I was brought up to it. I want something different for you. If you don't like your job, change it but don't think you can run away by coming back to me. You don't belong here any more.

LYNNE I don't belong anywhere.

MOTHER Don't give me that. You've made your life. You live it. I'll not have you here, Lynne. Not at any price!

LYNNE Who's going to look after you?

MOTHER When the day comes I can't manage I shall go and live with our Pat. She's got her head screwed on has Pat. She'll not sacrifice herself for me and that's how it should be... besides she needs help with those kids. They're bright kids but they need direction. It's them that matter now.

LYNNE And so it goes on.

MOTHER What did you say?

LYNNE Nothing. Nothing at all.

Voice Downstairs, Ears Upstairs

David Luck

The Cast

Andrew

Peter

Nurse

Jill

Jeff

Mrs Verse

Dan

Voice Downstairs, Ears Upstairs

1 The dining-room (morning)

Andrew is sitting at the table writing to his mother. His father, Peter, is clearing up in the kitchen. Distant sounds of pots and pans.

ANDREW (*to himself; slowly as he reads what he has written*) Dear Mum, how are you? I am well. (*Even slower as he writes*) I hope . . . (*Calls*) Dad!

PETER (*from kitchen*) You called?

ANDREW (*not listening*) Dad!

PETER (*coming to kitchen door – vigorously*) Hullo!

ANDREW How do you spell 'hope'?

PETER How do you think you spell it?

ANDREW I don't know. I've just written it.

PETER Well, if you've just written it why don't you read it to see what it says?

ANDREW It says 'hope'. Doesn't it?

PETER Let me have a look.

ANDREW Doesn't it? I'm writing to my Mum.

PETER That's very thoughtful of you. I don't think there's a 'y' in hope.

ANDREW (*quietly*) Dad?

PETER Yes.

ANDREW Mum's all right really, isn't she, what she's having done to her in the hospital?

PETER Yes. It's what Mums have done to them when they're in hospital.

ANDREW She won't have to go back again though, will she?

PETER ladies' insides.

ANDREW Dad?

PETER Yes.

ANDREW Is it her . . . is it her insides?

PETER Up to a point. And Andrew – chaps never refer to ladies' insides.

ANDREW (*giggles*) I know.

PETER (*mock serious*) It's not funny!

ANDREW (*quite loudly, trying not to laugh*) I know!

PETER (*returning to kitchen*) Well then, I hope – 'h' 'o' 'p' 'e' – you'll remember, that's all. Now finish off your letter while I'm hosing down the kitchen.

ANDREW (*reads to himself*) Dear Mum, how are you? I am well. (*Even slower as he writes*) I hope . . . I hope . . .

He screws up the letter.

(*Exasperated*) Oh!

2 The hospital at visiting time (afternoon: a subdued atmosphere)

PETER Excuse me. I'm looking for Mrs Walsh. She was in the other ward but they sent me over here.

NURSE Yes. They usually come to us afterwards. Now, let's see if we can find her shall we?

PETER Yes, please, if it's convenient.

Peter and Nurse walk through the ward.

NURSE (*calls*) I'll be with you in a moment, Mrs Bellamy. (*To Peter*) How are you coping looking after your little boy?

PETER We haven't got a little boy. Yes we have! We're managing the best we can. Thank you.

NURSE It's the little ones they miss the most. Now, not too much excitement. Here we are, Mrs Walsh, someone to see you.

PETER Thank you.

There is a brief pause as the nurse walks away.

Hullo.

He kisses Jill and sits by the bedside.

How are you?

JILL Rotten. It feels as if they've taken my stomach away . . . with something jagged.

PETER Is that how you should feel?

JILL That seems to be the general opinion.

PETER Is that what the doctors have told you?

JILL No. It's what we girls have decided.

PETER Some of the others have had it as well?

JILL Yes. Don't look so worried. I shall survive. And I'm pleased to see you.

PETER Yes. Well. Yes. I'm only sorry I couldn't bring our little one.

JILL I didn't know we had one.

PETER Nor me. The nurse seems to think I'm at home struggling with an infant. What have you been telling them?

JILL Nothing . . . that I remember.

PETER Perhaps you've blabbed under the anaesthetic. Mouthed ruderies?

JILL I could manage a few at the moment. You don't think I did, do you?

PETER You might have. Have a quick look round to see if anyone is smirking.

JILL I don't think I care very much. Even if I did. How is he?

PETER What, the little one? Much the same as usual. He sends his love.

JILL I thought he might come with you.

PETER No. I wanted to see how you were. I thought you might be feeling low and I thought it might upset him . . . and you.

JILL Bring him with you next time. I want to see him.

PETER He's as good as here. What will nurse say when she sees your little one is six foot tall with a moustache.

JILL A moustache! How did he manage that?

PETER I don't think he has yet. It may be a trick of the light.

JILL But he is all right?

PETER Of course. We have managed very well. There is nothing for you to worry about. (*After a moment*) There have been one or two minor incidents.

JILL What's happened? I knew there'd be something.

PETER Well. We've had a bit of a problem. Where do you keep the tea? We couldn't find it.

JILL Oh, you! (*Near to tears*) It's in the red tin.

PETER Are you all right?

JILL Can I have a tissue please? There's some on the locker.

Peter pulls out tissues.

PETER There you are. I promise you how ever long it takes and whatever the cost – we will find the tea.

JILL I'm sorry. I didn't mean to cry.

PETER I hardly noticed. I was still trying to see if anyone was smirking.

JILL I've made a list. You'll have to go to the supermarket this week. Take Andrew, he usually remembers where everything is. How have you been managing with your meals?

PETER Fine. No problems. We've had lots of things, like ... well, lots of things ...

3 The kitchen

ANDREW Hullo, Dad.

PETER Hullo, Andrew. Where've you been?

ANDREW Riding about on my bike. Did you know they've knocked down the building next to the park?

PETER No. I didn't know that.

ANDREW There's a big hole in the ground. Quite deep.

PETER Where's the fish and chips?

ANDREW In my saddlebag.

PETER Right, if you hold the door open, I'll take a couple of chairs outside. We can sit round your bike.

ANDREW What for?

PETER Eat our supper. You bring the vinegar.

ANDREW Don't be silly. I didn't go near the edge. So I wouldn't fall down the hole.

PETER Andrew, go and fetch the fish and chips.

Andrew walks through the hallway, to the garden.

PETER (*calling*) What do you keep in that saddlebag? Can't be as unsavoury as your bedroom. Can it? I don't think I really want to know.

ANDREW There you are.

He unwraps the parcel.

PETER What's this!

ANDREW Fish and chips.

PETER I can see that. What did you ask for?

ANDREW Twice. What you told me.

PETER There's only once here. And then only just.

ANDREW I've eaten mine.

PETER And half mine. Where's the change? (*firmly*) Andrew, where's the money?

ANDREW I've spent it. I bought some lemonade.

PETER So you've had a good time then?

ANDREW Yes. Thank you.

PETER This lot's stone cold.

ANDREW Well, you just put it in the oven. That's what Mum does.

PETER That's to keep them warm, not bring them back to life.

ANDREW That's what Mum does. Just warm them up.

PETER Are you sure that'll be all right?

ANDREW I think so. That's what Mum does.

PETER I'll give it a try, I'm starving.

He puts the fish and chips into the oven.

PETER In future I want you to go straight there and ... (*Shouts*) Andrew, come back here. (*Calls*) Perhaps I should buy you a ball and chain. One for each ear. (*Shouts*) Andrew! (*Calls*) Or a playpen. A metal one I can plug into the mains. (*Talks*) What have you been doing? Come here. What have you got on your head?

ANDREW It's that hair stuff. It keeps it in place.

PETER You've got some on your nose. Keeps that in place as well, doesn't it? Don't wipe it off on your sleeve. What do you think we've got wallpaper for?

ANDREW I wanted to look smart.

PETER You're not supposed to use the lot in one go.

ANDREW When I go and see Mum in hospital.

PETER I expect she'll think you look lovely.

ANDREW Yes.

PETER I thought you might think so. Go on. What else?

ANDREW I can tell her about Robin.

PETER Who's Robin?

ANDREW My pet rat.

PETER Is he with you now? About your person?

ANDREW No. Of course not. He's upstairs. In my bedroom.

PETER So that's it. How did he get there?

ANDREW I brought him. In my saddlebag.

PETER Turn the oven off, Andrew. Would you? Please.

ANDREW They won't be ready yet.

PETER I don't think I want them now.

ANDREW Can I give them to Robin?

ANDREW Go on then. I expect they're already rat-flavoured. And this is a last supper. You understand?

ANDREW No.

PETER He's got to go.

ANDREW Why?

PETER I'm not having livestock indoors. Your mother would have a fit if she knew.

ANDREW But she's not here.

PETER Serve Robin his supper.

He takes the plate out of the oven.

ANDREW He wouldn't be any trouble.

PETER He doesn't bite, does he?

ANDREW He's nice and clean.

PETER Oh! There's been a rodent in my bath!

ANDREW Yes. He enjoyed it. He can swim.

PETER Followed by a brisk rub down with a towel. No, don't tell me. Mind how you go upstairs with that.

ANDREW (*shouts from some distance*) I'm teaching him to roll over.

PETER (*loudly*) And my next guest is an illiterate ex-floor sweeper who teaches rats to roll over.

ANDREW (*calls from some distance*) Goodnight, everyone.

4 The interior of a hospital at visiting time (afternoon: a subdued atmosphere)

JILL Did you find out why his job fell through?

PETER Yes. Apparently he wasn't strong enough.

JILL To push a broom? I don't believe it. I don't know why they took him on if they had no intention of keeping him.

PETER They can say they tried. They also said he couldn't follow instructions.

JILL Oh, really! How do they sweep their factory floor? In formation? You'll have to renew his prescription this week.

PETER For pills that are supposed to help him concentrate?

JILL I still think he's strong enough to lift a broom.

PETER So do I. But I think he may have forgotten what they told him to do.

JILL I wonder how hard they tried.

PETER It can't be easy. Not with him.

JILL But they're meant to take on people who are...

PETER Disabled? He's as sound in wind and limb as you are. Or will be. He's not the brightest person I've met.

JILL That's not the point.

PETER Although we would admit we might be biased.

JILL I suppose so. He's still going to his class, isn't he?

PETER Yes. Seems to be doing fine. He's got a new tutor. But he's coming on... I think they're quite pleased with him.

5 The kitchen

ANDREW Hullo, Dad.

PETER What have you got behind your back?

ANDREW Shut your eyes.

PETER Am I going to enjoy this?

ANDREW It's a surprise.

PETER Not horrible is it?

ANDREW Shut your eyes. There you are. That's my name and address. I've written it.

PETER That's very good. What's this bit. After your name?

ANDREW It says Andrew Walsh and Robin Rat.

PETER And did he write 'and Robin Rat'? Because if he did he can't spell. How do you spell 'and'?

ANDREW 'A'...'N'...'D'.

PETER Why don't you write it then?

ANDREW I don't know.

PETER But apart from that, how are you getting on?

ANDREW Janet says I'm doing very well.

PETER What happened to Maureen?

ANDREW She left to get a job. Something to do with trains.

PETER Driving them or what?

ANDREW I don't know.

PETER How about your homework? Have you done it yet?

ANDREW Up to a point.

PETER You've got to have it ready for tomorrow, haven't you? Shall I test you on it?

ANDREW Later on.

PETER You haven't started it yet, have you?

ANDREW Yes I have.

PETER What is it then?

ANDREW Writing.

PETER Brilliant. Well it couldn't be spelling, now could it.

ANDREW Why not?

PETER Because you can't, can you!

ANDREW Yes I can. Sometimes.

PETER Spell 'Andrew' for me. 'Andrew'.

ANDREW 'A' . . . 'A' . . .

PETER That's two 'A's. Very good.

ANDREW You're looking at me.

PETER Go on.

ANDREW 'A' . . . 'N' . . .

PETER What a looney.

ANDREW You mustn't say that!

PETER It's right though, isn't it?

ANDREW You wouldn't say that if Mum was here.

PETER Good job she's not. "And Janet says I'm doing very well!" What's the writing you've got to do?

ANDREW I've got to copy something.

PETER Go and get your books. (*calls*) Andrew. Come here.

ANDREW Yes?

PETER I suppose rat could live in the yard. If we made a cage or something. To put him in.

ANDREW With his name on it?

PETER If you like. Perhaps I'd better do that for you.

ANDREW Tomorrow?

PETER Yes. Now go and get your books.

6 The hospital at visiting time (afternoon)

PETER That reminds me. The lad has sent a letter for you.

JILL Are you going to give it to me or is it that illegible? You did say his lessons were going well.

PETER That's not the problem. In fact his writing's too legible. You're going to be able to read what he's written. And find out what he's been doing.

JILL And what has he been doing? That you'd rather I didn't know about?

PETER Well. He's had an accident on his bicycle and he's eaten a rubber glove.

JILL (*giggles*) I mustn't laugh.

PETER Does it hurt?

JILL Yes. But is he all right?

PETER Of course he is. He's indestructible.

JILL (*loudly*) A rubber glove!

PETER Shhhh! You'll have them all smirking again. If you promise to keep quiet I'll give you my version and then you can read his. Promise?

JILL Mmmmmmm.

PETER This won't be too exciting for you, will it?

JILL Mmmmmmm.

PETER Well just be careful that's all. The bike. He was coming home from his lesson when he hit a car.

JILL What happened! Was it parked without lights? Didn't he see it?

PETER It was parked without lights but then it was in someone's drive. And he didn't see it because he had his eyes shut.

JILL What on earth was he doing? He must have hurt himself.

PETER It's his new hobby. Going as fast as he can downhill with his eyes shut. The road bent, he didn't, the bike did. And he didn't feel a thing. Although I think he was surprised to open his eyes and find himself trying to pedal an ornamental fir tree across someone's lawn.

JILL What did the people say?

PETER Well, I don't know what he said to them but they seemed to think it was their fault. Brought him home. And his bike. It just needed the handlebars straightening. They were most concerned.

JILL Perhaps they didn't have a licence for the fir tree. It was good of them to look after him. I wonder if they'd like a sweeper up. Tell me about the glove.

PETER I've bought you a new pair. The others sprang a

leak. I threw them away but Andrew had taken them out of the bin and had cut off the fingers. And then he was helping me get the dinner.

JILL What were you having?

PETER Cheese sandwiches.

JILL That was on Sunday.

PETER How did you know that?

JILL The fish and chip shop doesn't open on a Sunday.

PETER That's right. Very good.

JILL I'd better have the shopping list back.

PETER Why? We won't mind going. Be an experience, won't it?

JILL If you've been living off fish and chips there's no need to get more food in, is there?

PETER I don't know. We almost made a jelly.

JILL What happened to that?

PETER He drank it. Thought it was all right as well.

JILL But what happened with the glove?

PETER Funny you should ask me that. I can only think that in the rush to see the cowboy film glove and sandwich got mingled. You know how he eats. Like a mechanical excavator. One mighty chomp and his gnashers are embedded in sandwich and glove. Just as the sheriff lost his posse there's a thwack of snapping rubber. There's bread and cheese everywhere and Andrew with a shredded yellow finger hanging out of his mouth. And that's when he drank the jelly. So you see there's been nothing at all for you to worry about.

JILL I wonder if you should be the one taking the pills. Is it safe for me to read this letter now?

PETER Yes. Of course. We have nothing to hide.

ANDREW (*reads slowly*) Dear Mum, how are you? I am well. I hope you are well. I fell off my bike in someone's garden and I eat a glove.

JILL He's written it nicely, hasn't he?

ANDREW (*reads slowly*) I hope you will be home soon. The weather is nice.

JILL (*reads*) Lots of love from Andrew. P.S. You will see my . . . What's a rad?

PETER (*quietly*) I think that's meant to be 'rat'.

JILL Sorry! A what?

PETER A rat.

7 The garden

Jeff is sawing. At some distance a door slams. Peter approaches.

PETER Keeping busy then, Jeff?

Jeff stops sawing.

JEFF You noticed.

PETER What's it going to be?

JEFF Only your woodlander table.

PETER Sounds most attractive. What sort of wood have you got?

JEFF Elm. I intend being buried in this table.

PETER Is is safe to eat off elm? I thought it was supposed to be diseased.

JEFF Of course it's safe. Unless you're another tree.

PETER Why do you want to be buried in it?

JEFF I don't want to be. I just thought it would save a bob or two. When the time came. They make coffins out of it. Elm.

PETER I could use some of that, if you have any left over.

JEFF There won't be enough for another picnic table.

PETER I only want enough to make a hutch for Andrew's new pet.

JEFF Yes? What's he got?

PETER A rat.

JEFF Going up market! I'd better trade in the mouse. Where did he get it?

PETER I haven't dared ask. I assumed it arrived with the old loudspeaker he found. I think he routs through unattended dustbins.

JEFF Does he! We'll have to be a bit more selective in what we throw away. I think I've still got an old cage of Darren's. He used to keep rabbits until he discovered girls.

PETER Andrew hasn't discovered rabbits.

JEFF Rats could be a start.

ANDREW (*calls at some distance*) Dad! Dad!

PETER Come and say hullo.

ANDREW (*approaching*) Hullo, Dad. Hullo, Mr Walters.

JEFF Hullo, Andrew.

PETER Have you got your pills?

ANDREW Yes. I fell off my bike.

JEFF Not in the chemist's!

PETER Show me what you've got.

ANDREW Well, I think I may have grazed my elbow.

PETER From the chemist!

ANDREW I've put them in the bathroom cabinet. Keep all medicines out of the reach of children.

JEFF Wear something white at night.

PETER And if we all join hands we'll see if anyone's there.

JEFF They might know where the hutch is.

ANDREW What's that?

PETER Mr Walters said he might have a hutch for Robin to live in. It's a cage. What do you say?

ANDREW Thank you very much, Mr Walters.

JEFF You're welcome. You can come and help me find it. (*To Peter*) If that's all right.

PETER Yes. Thanks. (*To Andrew*) But first you'd better get your old clothes on.

ANDREW I'll be careful.

PETER You've already fallen off your bike. That's meant to be your best suit. You haven't damaged it, have you?

ANDREW No. I gave it a wipe.

PETER Terrific. Now go and change. And don't forget to hang your suit up.

ANDREW All right. I won't be a minute. Don't go away anyone.

Andrew runs to the house. The back door slams.

JEFF He's a bit of a card your lad, isn't he?

PETER Something like that.

JEFF How's your good lady going on then?

PETER Not too bad I suppose. I'll find out this afternoon.

JEFF Are you taking the boy?

PETER No. Not until I know how she is.

JEFF I expect he's missed her.

From some distance a door slams and Andrew runs down the garden.

PETER Yes, although you can't always tell!

ANDREW I'm ready.

PETER Andrew, go and hang your suit up.

ANDREW I have.

PETER You couldn't have done it that quickly.

ANDREW Yes I could.

PETER You wouldn't have been able to find a hanger. And you've got your pullover on backwards. Now, go and hang your suit up and get dressed properly.

Andrew runs to the house and the door slams.

I'm not sure what to do with him. This afternoon.

JEFF He can stay with me, if you like. While you're visiting.

PETER That would be a help. It may retard the progress of your woodwork.

JEFF I don't know about that. He was the one who told me how to fix the fence post.

PEER You should have hit him with it.

JEFF How does he know about things like that? Things that have taken you and me years to get wrong.

PETER The sloping shelf.

JEFF The folding crockery cupboard.

PETER One of our more spectacular disasters.

JEFF Couldn't believe it was you and not the boy.

PETER I could have had him locked up if it had been.

JEFF I don't see why. We pass for normal. Sometimes.

The door slams and Andrew runs to them.

PETER Is that what it is. Anyway, thanks. It'll give me a chance to run a shovel over the carpet before I go.

ANDREW Is is all right if I get Mr Walters' hutch please, Dad?

PETER Yes, off you go.

JEFF Come round now, son, and we'll look for it.

PETER Go on then. Not over the fence. Go round, not over.

8 The hospital at visiting time (afternoon)

JILL It was good of Jeff to look after him this afternoon.

PETER Yes.

JILL You have told him to keep his eyes open when he's out on his bike?

PETER Yes.

JILL I've told you about the clean shirts.

PETER Yes.

The bell rings for the end of visiting time.

JILL And you'll bring him with you tonight?

PETER Yes.

JILL I'll see you later then.

PETER Yes.

JILL You have to go now. They've rung the bell.

PETER Yes.

JILL Haven't you got anything else to say?

Sounds of visitors leaving.

PETER Yes. (*Loudly*) It's been lovely seeing you again, Mrs Walsh. And, once again, I do assure you that the experiments on your son have been entirely successful.

JILL Ssshhhhhh.

PETER ... The puny three year old you remember dandling on your knee will stride through those doors this evening...

JILL Peter!

PETER ... transformed almost overnight into a mature six footer wearing, if the light's right, a moustache.

9 The kitchen

ANDREW (*shouts*) Dad! Dad!

PETER (*calls*) What? What?

Andrew comes in.

ANDREW Robin has gone!

PETER What do you mean?

ANDREW He's not in his cage.

PETER Picked the lock, did he?

ANDREW I don't know.

PETER Did you leave it open?

ANDREW I don't remember.

PETER He couldn't get out unless you did. And you've left the back gate open. Where've you been?

ANDREW I went for a walk. I wanted to get him some dock leaves.

PETER I think he would have appreciated that.

ANDREW Do you think he'll be all right?

PETER I expect so. He's probably down the refuse dump teaching his mates to roll over.

ANDREW Where's that?

PETER Where's what?

ANDREW What you said. That place.

PETER The refuse dump?

ANDREW Yes.

PETER Where we took our old cooker. Just over the canal. But I don't think he's there. More likely to come back here for a warm and a feed.

ANDREW I hope so.

PETER So do I. Gosh, I do miss that rat. I wonder if you have any idea how much I miss that rat? But in the meantime. How about a nice wash? And remember to take off your gloves.

ANDREW I'm not wearing gloves.

PETER In that case I think you should do something about your hands. Har, har, har, and your neck. I think we'll do the ears while we're at it.

ANDREW Oh, no, you always hurt.

PETER The one you love. But then you want to look lovely for your Mum, don't you?

ANDREW Am I going to see her? Is she better? Is she coming home?

PETER Yes, yes and yes. Now go and get ready and no playing about.

ANDREW No I won't. I shall be very quick just you wait and see.

10 The garden

PETER (*calls*) Jeff!

JEFF (*approaching*) Now then. What news?

PETER Oh fine thanks.

JEFF Yes, but who?

PETER Sorry, well, in order of height – son: getting ready

for evening visit to Mum. Father: thanking neighbour for caring for son.

JEFF Neighbour: eyes brown downcast, medium height, looking modest.

PETER And rat, same colour eyes – missing.

JEFF Perhaps he didn't have enough room to roll over.

PETER He told you.

JEFF Yes. Still, I think a boy should have an interest.

PETER He wasn't any trouble?

JEFF No, of course not. Pity about the rat though.

PETER I could always get him a rabbit.

JEFF I'm not so sure, look what it did to my Darren, spotty little pagan. Anyway, how's the ex-rat trainer's Mummy?

PETER Fragile but claims to be looking forward to seeing son. Which reminds me. I'll see you later, and thanks again.

11 Inside the house

PETER (*calls*) Andrew! (*pause*) Andrew?

He goes upstairs.

Andrew, how much longer are you going to be? I hope you're not still in the bathroom. (*calls*) Andrew!

A door opens.

I'll kill him! I'm going to kill him!

12 The hospital ward

MRS VERSE I expect your boy will be getting excited at the thought of seeing you.

JILL Yes, I expect so.

MRS VERSE He's still at school, isn't he?

JILL No. He . . . no, he left.

MRS VERSE Oh, I thought I heard you talking to your husband about his lessons.

JILL No, not those lessons. My son's illiterate. He's still being taught to read and write.

MRS VERSE My Cyril was a slow learner. Takes after his father. Your husband seems a lively sort of man.

JILL That's narrowed the field. Well, yes, I do have trouble spelling. Words like gladiator and eucharist.

MRS VERSE Oh, you're a keen gardener then?

JILL Mmmmmmm!

MRS VERSE Do you want the nurse, dear?

JILL No. No thank you.

MRS VERSE I expect you'll buck up when your visitors arrive.

13 The garden

PETER I'll kill him. I'm going to kill him!

JEFF You mean he's not in the house anywhere?

PETER I've looked.

JEFF Well, he didn't come out this way. Unless he wriggled past on his stomach.

PETER It's possible.

JEFF Not when he's all dolled up to see his Mum, surely? He may have come out this way then! Look, he can't have gone far. He knew he was going to see his Mum.

PETER He will have forgotten.

JEFF Have you any idea where he might have gone? Perhaps he's gone on to the hospital?

PETER The refuse tip.

JEFF Can't say I'd have thought of that, despite the similarities. I'll get the car out. Come on.

14 The hospital ward

MRS VERSE Well I still think you're brave to keep on with him. It must be a trial for you at times.

JILL It's not that bad. We have our lighter moments.

MRS VERSE I'm sure you do.

JILL Although he may have made us unpopular with the postman.

MRS VERSE Why? He doesn't bite, does he?

JILL No, of course not. We were getting rather a lot of post. He'd just learnt to write his name and address. So at every opportunity he did. Sent off for things. Mail order catalogues. Holiday brochures. We've had the offer of a free survey for woodworm.

MRS VERSE I do that.

JILL Survey woodworm?

MRS VERSE No, dear. Send away for things. That's how I got my bedjacket. I think it was made by Australian refugees.

JILL It suits you.

MRS VERSE And a thing you can make ashtrays with.

JILL I haven't seen you smoke.

MRS VERSE I don't. How did he know what he was getting?

JILL He didn't. He just recognised the words 'name' and 'address' and filled them in.

MRS VERSE Life's full of little surprises. As my Bernard always used to say.

15 The refuse dump

DAN I don't know. He might have been. We get all sorts in here.

JEFF It would have been, what, within the last half hour.

DAN What's he look like then?

PETER Tall, thin, big hands and his ears stick out.

JEFF And his suit may be a bit muddy.

DAN I know him. Sells gas stoves.

PETER Used to have a pet rat.

DAN Don't know about that. There's a woman comes in to see our new crusher.

JEFF Doesn't sound like him.

PETER Come on, I should be at the hospital by now.

Peter and Jeff walk away from Dan.

DAN (*fading*) If you ever want a gas stove . . . or a fridge.

JEFF (*calls*) Thanks. (*To Peter*) What will you tell Jill?

PETER I don't know. Can we go home first? He may have turned up there.

16 The hospital at visiting time (evening: noisier than the afternoons)

MRS VERSE Well if you haven't got a car then I suppose they've missed their bus.

JILL Yes, that could be it.

MRS VERSE They have music on our buses.

JILL I suppose it gives the conductors something to do.

MRS VERSE They have advertisements as well. But only upstairs. I only listen to the music. Do they have it on yours?

JILL No, I don't think so.

MRS VERSE It's probably only on select routes like mine. There are a lot in tonight. I expect yours will be strolling in any minute now. Without a care in the world. Men are all the same. Just like my Bernard was.

17 The house

PETER (*calls*) Andrew! Andrew?
He goes upstairs.
Andrew!

ANDREW (*loudspeaker voice*) Dad!

PETER Andrew, where are you?

ANDREW (*loudspeaker voice*) Dad?
Peter climbs the rest of the stairs.

PETER Where are you?

ANDREW (*loudspeaker voice*) I'm up here.

PETER But I can hear you downstairs.

ANDREW (*loudspeaker voice*) My voice is downstairs but I'm up here.

PETER And your ears are upstairs so will you please tell me exactly where you are?

ANDREW (*loudspeaker voice*) I'm in the attic.

Peter mounts the attic stairs and pushes up the trap door.

ANDREW The trap door got stuck and I couldn't get out.

PETER The last time I saw you, you were supposed to be getting ready to see your Mother.

ANDREW I wanted to give you a shock.

PETER Thanks.

ANDREW I'd say "Hullo Dad" when you came in and you wouldn't know where I was.

PETER I didn't hear you say "Hullo Dad".

ANDREW I didn't know when you'd come in.

PETER When I'd come in when?

ANDREW To take me to see Mum.

PETER But I was shouting. You must have heard me.

ANDREW Well, yes, but I was trying to stop myself from laughing.

PETER I think I almost understand. But why was your voice downstairs? How did you do that?

ANDREW I found a loudspeaker and I've connected it up to my recorder.

Pause.

PETER But you don't even know about rabbits yet.

18 The hospital (evening visiting)

ANDREW (*approaching*) Hullo, Mum. We're here.

JILL Hullo. Have you missed me?

ANDREW Yes. I got stuck in the attic and Dad went down the rubbish tip to look for me.

JILL Why was that?

PETER We've missed you.

ANDREW Mr Walters is going to be buried in a table.

PETER We've missed you. I wonder if you have any idea how much we've missed you?.

ANDREW You said that about Robin Rat, didn't you, Dad?

JILL I'm feeling much better already.

PETER (*to Andrew*) Spell 'rat'.

ANDREW 'R' . . . 'A' . . . 'T'. I fell off my bike at the chemist's.

PETER I told you he was alright.

JILL Yes. It sounds as if I've been away for years.

PETER No, he's just told you everything at once.
ANDREW And I've torn my best trousers.
PETER Almost everything.

It's A Wise Child

Wally K. Daly

The Cast

Local Adjudicator

Guv

Eddie

Fred

Kev

Bret

Kitty

Norm

Kev's Mum

Driver

Madelaine

Ethel

Aunt Violet

Porter

London Adjudicator

It's A Wise Child

1 A large hall packed with people (mainly young)

Background of shuffles as the Adjudicator speaks.

LOCAL ADJUDIC. ... and I must say further that the standard of this particular finals has been among the highest that I've ever known ...

Ad libbed "Hear hear"s.

... so this makes doubly difficult the task that now faces me. Out of the sixteen local finalists from Boys' Clubs, Girls' Clubs and Mixed Clubs who have performed their one act plays for us today – only one can go forward to represent the Northern area in the London finals and it's my unenviable task to be the one who picks that finalist. From where I'm standing I can see a lot of tension on a lot of young faces ...

Laughter.

... so I'll now put you all out of your misery ...

Laughter.

... I'll just repeat – this is a personal choice on my part. Lots of you will have your own particular favourites and may disagree with my choice, but I'm sure in a sportsman-like way applaud the winners. It is a close run decision. So close in fact that I'm going to break with tradition and announce the winner first rather than those placed third and second. The winner of the Northern Area Finals of the National Association of Boys' and Girls' Clubs, who will now go forward to compete with the other area finalists in a grand final in London, to find the club drama group of the year, is – Grangebank Boys' Club!

Tumultuous cheers and applause.

2 A small office

Noise of boys' club activities and boys' voices held in distance.

GUV (*on telephone*) ... well it's very nice of you to say so, Mr Wight ... yes it was one of those moments – I was proud to be the leader ... No, your driver was very helpful – led the sing-song on the way home ... Yes ... you can book the coach straight down again now if you like ... Oh – how many seats is that one? ... Cost a packet more I suppose? ... Very kind of you – very kind indeed. That's a big help. We'll be able to sell the extra seats to supporters, keep the average cost down ... yes – out of their own pockets ... No, I realise that – you run a business. Good of you to give us the larger coach at the same cost.

Knock on door.

Right, Mr Wight, many thanks again. 'Bye.

He puts the phone down. Knock on door.

Come.

Pause – another knock.

Come in.

Long pause – louder knock.

Come in!

Door opens.

EDDIE Can I come in, Guv?

GUV I said come in.

EDDIE Pardon?

GUV I said ... Eddie. What are you playing at?

EDDIE I'll come in then.

Door closing.

GUV Sit down, Eddie.

EDDIE Can I sit down, Guv?

GUV I've just said ... (*Amazed*) You've got cotton wool in your ears.

EDDIE Sorry, Guv, I can't hear very well – I've got cotton wool in my ears.

GUV Why have you got cotton wool in your ears, Eddie?

EDDIE What?

GUV Why have...? This is ridiculous even by Little Eddie standards. Let's get rid of the blockage and find out the plan.

He stands and crosses to Eddie.

EDDIE Ow! What do you do that for, Guv? You've spoilt it by taking them out.

GUV Spoilt what?

EDDIE My project.

GUV What project?

EDDIE My project to find out what it's like to have a different sort of disablement than mine...

GUV But you haven't...

EDDIE ...I've been deaf for half an hour now and it's awful – you wouldn't believe it, Guv – the kids in this club are very slovenly talkers. I can't make their lip movements out at all. You should talk to them about that.

GUV Well, that's very...

EDDIE Tomorrow evening I'm going to blindfold myself to see what it's like bei...

GUV Hang on, hang on, hang on. Let's start again. You're checking the inconvenience of other disablement...

EDDIE That's right – ever thought what it's like going up flights of stairs with only one leg? Now when ...

GUV It's still hang on time. So hang on. Why are you doing all this Eddie? I mean it's very nice to discover that if we all articulated better it would help deaf people: if it's that sort of reason it's a good idea, but experience tells me there's probably something else. What is it?

EDDIE Well I'm fed up of feeling sorry for myself with my disablement so I thought...

GUV Eddie, you haven't got a disablement. I've known you ever since you conned your way into this club when you were two years under age of admission. And in all the long hard years that have passed since then not the slightest trace of disablement have I noticed – the two weeks you lost your voice doesn't count though I remember it with pleasure – so what may I ask is your disablement?

EDDIE The fact that I'm an orphan.

GUV A disablement. The fact that you're an orphan. That's the biggest stroke of luck you've had in your life.

EDDIE How come?

GUV Whoever had the foresight to leave you in a carrier bag outside the Bottom House pub when you were a baby – not only must have had some strange premonition that you were going to turn into the world's greatest con man, but gave you the ammunition to pull it off as well...

EDDIE You're talking like a club leader again, Guv – you know I never understand you when you talk like a club leader...

GUV ... besides giving you the good fortune to be found by two unsuspecting people who've allowed you to twiddle them around your little finger ever since – they also made you small and amazingly appealing like something hard done by out of *Oliver Twist* – but it cuts no ice with me, Eddie – so get to the point. What are you after?

3 The entrance to the club

A motorbike approaches and stops. Fred opens the door.

FRED Wotcha, Kev!

KEV (*muted*) Hello, Fred.

FRED Good to see you again. Thought you'd given us up as a bad job.

KEV Naw. Been a bit tied up you know. Lot of overtime and things.

FRED Of course. Sorry to hear about your dad, Kev.

KEV Well – that's how it goes, Fred.

FRED Your mate Norm's been telling everyone about your holiday. Sounds great.

KEV Yeah. Okay. Is he in, Fred? Norm, I mean. I thought I might catch him here.

FRED Yeah – upstairs in the coffee bar, I think.

KEV Okay, I'll get up there. Time I congratulated the drama lot on their win as well. Are they rehearsing tonight?

FRED Yes. Oh that reminds me – Bret wants to see you.

KEV What for?

FRED Who knows, Kev, who knows. Now our lovable drama group leader has had greatness almost thrust upon him – he's even harder to fathom than usual – see you later.

KEV See you later, Fred.

4 Back in the office

GUV . . . Get – to – the – point – Eddie.

EDDIE Right, Guv. Shan't take up much more of your time – now I'm very fed up with being sorry for myself because of my affliction . . .

GUV Let's not get into that again. We'll take the commercial as being read. Just jump straight into the main feature.

EDDIE Okay. Now for reasons which I'd rather not disclose at the moment – it has become important that I go to London for a few days . . .

GUV Ah! Finally – not unlike St Paul on the road to Damascus I start to see a glimmer of light. (*Wonderingly*) I didn't see you in the play that won the competition did I, Eddie?

EDDIE No, Guv. I'm not in that one.

GUV Oh.

EDDIE It does seem that there's a little something missing there, doesn't it?

GUV Turned it down, didn't you?

EDDIE Yes. Too busy. Too busy. Now . . .

GUV No, hang on, now let's see – it's important you go to London for reasons which you'd rather not disclose at the moment. Right?

EDDIE Right.

GUV And you know there's a coach just happening to be going in that direction next weekend, right?

EDDIE Right.

GUV And you know the blokes in the play don't pay, but the supporters do. Right?

EDDIE Right.

GUV And you'd like to be on the coach – right?

EDDIE Right.

GUV But you can't afford to pay – right?

EDDIE (*amazed*) Right.

GUV And you want a free lift – as statistically there's one empty seat on any size coach, and you'll fill it for us absolutely without charge.

EDDIE Right!!! Guv – you're fantastic. That's just straightforward mind-reading without even a hint from me. Terrific! It's *you* who should be on the stage, Guv, not Bret's lot – you're incredible.

5 A rehearsal is in progress

A door opening.

KEV Oh! Sorry to interrupt.

BRET Hello, Kev. Just the man I wanted to see.

VOICES *General ad lib: "Hello, Kev", "Watcher, mate" etc.*

KEV I just called in to say congratulations on the win – I didn't mean to interrupt. Congratulations everyone.

General "Thank you"s.

BRET You're interrupting nowt, we're just breaking. Right. Snack time everyone. Five minutes for coffee and buns then back – I want to talk with Kev so you all clear out.

The boys leave the room. Gentle banter.

Sorry about your dad, Kev. Never knew him, but heard he was a nice bloke.

KEV Aye – all right I reckon – bit of a boozer, but – still that's done now. You wanted to see me, Bret?

BRET Yes. It's about the play. I'm in a bit of a hole. I know you couldn't do it when we started – lady trouble taking the time up, that sort of thing...

KEV (*laughs*) Yeah. Daphne. No trouble at the time, all fun – courting strong's turned into not talking I'm afraid. No problem now.

BRET That's love, Kev. Never smooth – ask the missus. Still, that's half my problem answered. How'd you feel about coming back in the play now you're unattached?

KEV Doing what? I mean no one's going to be daft enough to drop out now you've got a trip to London in the bag, are they? And I'd never take over if you dropped anyone – wouldn't be fair – they're all me mates.

BRET You know I'd never do owt like that this stage in the game, they're my mates as well. No – what's happened is that this "Ultimate Punishment" thing we're doing has got voices off, male and female, just odd comments added now and again, nowt flash but very important to the piece – and I've been doing the men and the missus has been doing the women, no problem – we're always there, seemed sensible at the time. We're always at the side and it's been allowed.

KEV Well – I can't see the problem. Sounds like a good arrangement.

BRET We've hit the big time, Kev. London finals – there's no way we can get away with it, it's got to be a member not a tutor. So I'm going to see if I can organise Madelaine from Loftborough Girls' Club to do the women's voices – and Kev me old mate, I want you to come out of retirement and tackle the men's voices – what do you say? It'll be hard work for a week getting it together but I reckon you could do it with both hands tied behind you. What do you say?

KEV Bret – best bit of news I've had since Daphne packed me up. Being honest, I've been as jealous as hell of the other blokes since you all won. Cheers me up no end, the chance of being one of the group again. I'll have to ask me mam like, but I can't see any problem. Bret – I think you've just got yourself some male voices off for London.

BRET Good lad, Kev. I knew you wouldn't let me down.

6 A busy public bar

Fred and Bret are having a drink.

BRET So what's keeping him, Fred?

FRED Last second phone call as we were locking up. He'll be along.

BRET Better be quick else his beer'll go cold.

FRED Aye – might miss his round as well; you know what a tragedy that'd be for Guv. (*Chuckles*)

They both drink.

FRED How'd it go tonight, Bret?

BRET Great. They've just about hit the peak. Rehearse them much more and they'll be over the top. I've drafted Kev in to do the odd voices so it takes the pressure off them a bit – I'll have to spend a lot of time getting him up to scratch.

FRED Aye. He was telling me. Quietly chuffed in his own little way, was our Kev. Had to battle to stop himself smiling. Funny that smiling business. He told me he nearly didn't come back 'cos he couldn't face the condolences and then when he got here nobody said next to nowt which was almost as bad. Couldn't work it out.

BRET Aye. Funny thing death when you're young.

FRED A laugh a minute when you're old, eh? (*Chuckles*)

BRET Not exactly, but you get to know the rules. Learn how to react to people's sorrow at your sorrow. You see what I mean?

FRED (*jokingly intense*) Learn to 'live' with 'death' as it were.

BRET Fred, you're a tyke. Never let anyone accuse you of having a serious conversation.

FRED All right, Bret – you're on.

BRET Tell you what – real confession night for Kev tonight all round, told me he wants to be an actor full time.

FRED Getta way!

BRET Straight up. Asked me what I thought.

FRED And what did you think?

BRET Well, he's come on a lot in the last few years and he'll soon have a trade to fall back on, but ...

The door opens.

FRED Hello! Look who's heading in our direction at forty scowls an hour.

GUV Surprise, surprise. Bret and Fred. How unusual meeting you here.

BRET Watcher, Guv. We were just going to drink your pint for you – help you out – knowing how overworked you are.

GUV I think I'll probably just manage it, thanks all the same, Bret. (*He drinks.*)

FRED Anyone exciting on the phone?

GUV Oh yes, Fred. The magnificent Ethel. Loftborough Girls' Club leader extraordinaire. "Congratulations on your win" – not even a whiff of sour grapes – "and we have decided at a meeting tonight, because of the close ties dramatically over the years between our clubs, that I and a few girls should come along to London and cheer you on".

FRED To which you replied, "Sorry, Ethel, no spare seats".

GUV To which I replied "Ethel, there would have been no spare seats, but tonight Mr Wight, Coaches Limited, off his own bat – unasked, at no extra expense, gave us a bigger coach with spare seats ..."

FRED What a rotten trick. That man Wight's really got it in for us.

GUV ... so we'd love to have you join us.

BRET That's handy.

GUV Handy! My marauding males loose in London's bad enough – plus Ethel's girls – is state of emergency stuff.

FRED You've got a wicked sense of humour, Bret, I'll give you that.

BRET Girls' voices off – remember?

GUV Girls' voices off remember? (*Pause*) No, remind me.

BRET The wife and I can't do the voices off – posh play – London premier – a maiden is required.

FRED From Loftborough?

BRET Madelaine. We need Madelaine.

GUV Gets worse and worse.

BRET I mean it, Guv – she's the best of the bunch.

FRED Certainly the biggest.

GUV Joking apart – I'd forgot the girls' voices. We can't get one of the young kids doing the falsetto bit?

BRET Not well enough to leave any chance of winning.

GUV Right. I'll ask Ethel. I'm sure it'll be all right.

BRET Good. I've got Kev doing the male bits so we're well covered all round now.

GUV (*slight pause*) Ah.

BRET Would you like to explain that "Ah", Guv? A lot of leadership doubt you're expressing there – no problem with Kev. I've checked.

GUV It's not Kev. Little Eddie was in to see me tonight – trying to fiddle a free ride to London – important business, no less. I told him "no way", unless he was part of the play...

FRED Oh, you're a hard man, Beadle.

GUV ... but – that I'd have a word with you about the voices off.

BRET (*slight pause*) Ah.

FRED You notice how Bret's "Ah" is much more dramatic than yours, Guv – years of training gone into his, you see – Don't worry boys, Fred will sort you out. I hereby resign as furniture shifter and prop boy on the masterpiece – Eddie can do it.

BRET I already thought of that – you're not allowed either – I sacked you tonight – I've asked Norm to do it and he accepted.

FRED (*slight pause*) Ah.

GUV Well – that's that then – I'll let him know tomorrow. No free trip.

BRET I couldn't do that to you, Guv – even I couldn't do that to you – I can just see those spaniel eyes of his misting over, then the big brave smile – extra hard swallow – (*He swallows hard*) – and "It's all right, Guv. Didn't really want to go this weekend". Couldn't do that to you. No – four assorted male voices off required, obviously a two-man job. Kev can do the low ones – Eddie the high ones. Okay?

GUV Okay. Good. That's that settled. Half pint each, right?

BRET (*amazed*) You're a worse con man than Eddie! You knew all the time I couldn't turn him down.

GUV (*moving away*) 'Course I did. Who can turn Eddie down? Three halves, pet.

FRED Here, Bret. I've got a bone to pick with you. How come you sacked me from my job without notice . . . ?

7 A café

The juke box is playing in the background. Kev arrives on his motorbike. The door bangs open.

KEV (*speaking above the noise*) Hello, Kitty!

KITTY Hello, Kev. How are you, love?

KEV Fine. Norm in?

KITTY Far corner, with Eddie.

KEV Oh yeah. I see.

KITTY Coffee, pet?

KEV Please.

Kev makes his way through the café.

Watcher, Norm.

NORM Hi, Kev. Look who I found in a big polythene bag outside the club.

KEV Hi, Eddie.

EDDIE Lo, Kev.

NORM How'd your mam take the news about London, Kev?

KEV Great – no problem. How about yours?

NORM The same. I told her you were going – and there's no way she's going to let your mam get one up on her, so it was guaranteed no grumbles. Eddie tells me he's going as well.

KEV Oh good.

EDDIE Yeah. Got to go to London on some business. Guv's making me work my passage for a free seat.

KEV What're you doing?

EDDIE Voices off or summat – Guv's checking with Bret.

KEV Are you sure? Bret asked me to do the voices off tonight.

EDDIE Well – there's loads of voices – girls as well.

KEV Madelaine from Loftsborough being booked to do the girls' voices . . .

EDDIE/NORM Great!

KEV . . . so I can't see what's left.

EDDIE Don't worry about it, Kev – probably 'cos your voice's broke. Funny – you'll get the deep ones to do – all the baddies. I'll probably get all the goodies, as my voice is still all right – but I do think they need another girl as well, to keep it balanced – you know – more my size like. So I better talk to Bret about that when he asks me to be in it.

NORM You're about as subtle as a sledgehammer, Eddie. You'll never swing that.

EDDIE Worth a try, though, isn't it?

NORM Not half! Reckon I can have one to help with the props?

EDDIE (*confident*) Yes. What size do you want?

Kitty brings the coffee.

KITTY Here you are, Kev – on the slate?

KEV Yes. Thanks, Kitty. Pay you Friday?

KITTY Okay, pet.

NORM So what's all this "business" you've got to attend to in London, Eddie?

EDDIE Well. I don't really want to talk about it...

NORM Okay.

EDDIE ... but as it's Kev who got me thinking about it, I suppose I could tell you both – in confidence like.

KEV Got you thinking about what?

EDDIE About my old man.

KEV I don't get you.

EDDIE Your dad dying. I mean you knew, didn't you? Were sort of prepared for it. Everyone knew for ages he was going to snuff it, didn't they?

NORM (*quiet*) Careful, Eddie.

EDDIE Naw. I'm not putting Kev down, Norm. You know what I mean, Kev. It happens; it hurts; you face it and have to live with it – but at least you know. See what I mean? I have no way of knowing.

KEV Well your old man's all right. I saw him behind the counter in the shop only this afternoon – right as rain.

EDDIE Aw come on, Kev. That's not my dad – you know that same as everyone else does. Why do you think we get on so well together? Naw, I'm talking about me real dad – and me real mam come to that.

NORM Well who are they?

EDDIE I don't know. Reckon I might find out in London.

NORM Well you can't just tap seven million people on the shoulder and say "Excuse me are you my mam or dad?" – I mean, how you going to find out?

EDDIE Not sure. There's a place down there that deals with adopted kids finding out – I'll try them. I got the number off directory enquiries.

NORM Yes but... why, Eddie? I mean – you've come out about the best of any of the kids in Vaughan Street. Let's face it. My old man's a misery. Kev's old man was a boozer. The one you've got is the only reasonable one out of the bunch of them. If you could adopt parents he's the one we'd all pick. I mean your *real* ones might be really grotty for all you know. Apparently it was a very tatty bag they left you in.

EDDIE I know that. I know all that. But I've still got to try and find them. Find where they live.

NORM Why?

EDDIE (*long pause*) Because if I don't know where they live, how can I know when they die?

NORM (*quiet*) I don't get it. I really don't get it, Ed.

KEV (*pause*) I do. (*Pause*) Have you had a talk with your mam and dad about it?

EDDIE Naw. Don't like to upset 'em. I'll wait till I get to London. I'm going to stay with me Aunty Vi on the outskirts for a couple of nights. I'll have a chat with her about it. She was living round here at the time.

KEV Yeah. Well – we'll be there. Owt we can do to help let us know. Right, Norm?

NORM Right. Yeah sure...

EDDIE That's nice – ta – take you up on that.

NORM Mind you – I still don't get it...

8 Kev's house

The back door opens.

KEV (*distant*) Me, mam! In the kitchen?

MAM Yes, son. Through here. Tea's all ready.

He sits down at the table and his mother serves the meal.

KEV Good. Get it down me and I'll be off. Last rehearsal tonight. Going really good.

MAM Your stuff's all packed – extra socks and clean pyjamas; all ready for the off tomorrow.

KEV Ta, mam. Can't wait to get there. Going to look round a couple of drama schools while I'm there – see how they work like. Bret reckons I might be able to get a grant if I play me cards right.

MAM Grant for what, son?

KEV Drama school.

MAM You've lost me, Kev. Sorry, son. Old age or something, I'm not with you at all.

KEV Well – perhaps I'm spelling it out wrong. I've been meaning to tell you for a while – but didn't know how to go about it really. I think I'm trying to say – (*Pause*) – I want to be an actor, mam – go to school for it like.

MAM An actor?

KEV Yeah.

MAM What – full-time?

KEV That's the idea. Go to drama school for a couple of years, learn how to do it proper, then become an actor. What do you think?

MAM Seems a bit strange really, son. Bit unexpected.

KEV Nowt strange about it – loads of people do it.

MAM Aye, but not from the works, son – you don't get that many blokes off the south plant going off to be actors, now do you?

KEV I think *I'm* going to, mam, strange or not.

MAM Well, Kev – what you do when you're out of your time's your own affair, but . . .

KEV I was thinking I might pack it up – me trade like. Pack it up, get a grant and go to school – drama school.

MAM Oh no, son! You can't do owt that daft. What would your dad think? He was so proud at the thought of having a tradesman in the family. You can't pack it up this near to being finished – it's unfair to him.

KEV I *can* pack it up. I'm not indentured or owt. Anyway – what's so special about having a trade? I've been nowt but cheap labour for the last year. You know that. Man's work for boy's money. Bit of overtime off Ernie to keep me sweet 'cos he knows it's wrong. But I don't think it's any good. I know I want out, mam. Out of Vaughan Street. Out of the works – you know that. I think I've found a way. I want to be an actor.

MAM And I know what your dad said: "A tradesman in the family – we're coming on."

KEV (*angry*) Don't keep wrapping him round me

neck like the bloody albatros. Get him off me. I'm *me.* Can't you see that? He talked about conveyor belt lives as well. Well, I want off. Now! Can't you see that? I'm playing his games and life's too short. Mam. This is me. An unhappy bloke battling to make a dead man's dreams come true! It's stupid. Can't you see? It's stupid. (*Long pause*) Sorry. I'm sorry, mam. Bit carried away.

MAM No, son. You're probably right. Kids are like toys to us parents. But instead of us parents growing too old for our toys – our toys grow too old for us parents. You're a man now. I'd lost sight of that. Make your own decisions, Kev. I'll help you all I can. The trade's nowt but your dad's dream. And he's as dead as dead. Be an actor, son, if that's what you want.

9 Outside the club

The sound of the coach ticking over. Voices in the background.

GUV That it, Fred?

FRED That's it, Guv, all present and correct.

GUV Okay, driver! Off we go.

DRIVER Right.

Sliding door slams shut. Coach revs up and starts off.

GUV (*calling*) All right – nice big wave to any mams and dads out there, lads. They all know in their heart of hearts that they'll never see any of you again and that it was a terrible mistake letting you go to the wicked city. So give 'em all a last big smile. Okay?

General laughter and chat and shouted "Goodbyes". General settling down noises.

GUV Budge up a bit, Fred.

FRED Right.

Guv sits.

GUV Well, that wasn't too painful.

FRED No. Fine. On our way at last.

GUV (*calling*) All right, Bret?

BRET (*distant*) Fine, Guv.

GUV Right. Well, Fred, what do you reckon – crossword time?

FRED Aye. Do the junior one first, shall we?

GUV Naw. Save it up for when Ethel and her lot get on. Do it quick like, try to impress...

Very close, voice singing "Show Me The Way To Go Home".

...We've been set off 30 seconds and a voice like a corncrake's bawling "Show me the way to go home", two foot away from my ear, Fred. I wonder who that could be?

FRED I wouldn't have the slightest idea, Guv.

GUV Evening, Eddie.

Eddie stops singing.

EDDIE Oh. Hello, Guv. Thought I'd get the singing started early – make the time pass; boring travelling, isn't it?

GUV You don't think it might be better getting it started from the back of the coach, do you, Eddie? Let it slowly filter up here like.

EDDIE Naw – I think it's best to get it started from the front of the coach, Guv, and let it slowly filter down there like. Mind you, there are different schools of thought. Still, I've got to sit up here, in any case, 'cos this is where you are. Biggest on the coach, you see.

GUV Ah. Would you excuse me for a moment, Fred. I think I'm about to receive a little more education.

FRED Certainly, Guv'nor. I'll get the hard bits of the crossword out of the way while you're gone – save you the bother.

GUV Budge up, Ed, I'll sit next to you.

Guv stands.

EDDIE Ah, you've spoilt it now. It's no good sitting "next" to the biggest – you've got to be "behind" him otherwise it doesn't work.

GUV (*long pause*) I bet you explain it finally if I wait long enough.

EDDIE (*long pause*) Right. You're sat behind a small

person – any vehicle – the crash happens "Smash!" you're straight over their heads, right? Landing on hard bits, hurting all over. You're sat behind a big person – the crash happens "Smash!" and he acts as a nice soft buffer between you and the hard bits...

GUV Oh. Thank you very much.

EDDIE ...particularly if he's well padded – like you, Guv.

GUV What do you mean, well padded?

EDDIE Well – no offence – but you have been putting on a bit of weight these last few years, Guv. When I joined this club as a kid, you used to be like a whippet. Still, not to worry, when the Loftborough lot get on I'll sit behind Ethel. Give you a break. She's even better than you are.

GUV Don't you dare say owt like that to her, Little Eddie. I've got enough problems.

EDDIE Wouldn't dream of it, Guv, unless she asks me of course. I'm ever so diplomatic really. Have you never noticed?

GUV I probably wasn't looking closely, Ed.

EDDIE Oh I am. Talking about being diplomatic, Guv. When me Aunt Vi meets me at the other end, you won't laugh when you hear her talk, will you?

GUV Why on earth should I laugh when I hear her talk?

EDDIE Well – she talks a bit posh like – bit like a woman newsreader. Can't help it mind – apparently everyone starts talking daft if they leave Grangebank for any length of time.

GUV She a Grangebank lass, then?

EDDIE Aye – me dad's sister. Came up years ago – married a bloke here – me uncle like. Got a couple of kids now, real savages – can't understand a word they say. Still – they think I'm great and that's the important thing, isn't it?

GUV Oh. Aye, it would be. While we're at it – you're going to make sure you get to the theatre on time and things, and back for the bus, Sunday?

EDDIE Would I let you down, Guv? Aunt Vi's got a car – dead posh, you see – she's going to make sure I get everywhere on time.

GUV Right. Well – I'd better get back to the crossword.

EDDIE Good idea.

The sound of the coach builds up and then fades down as we focus on Kev and Norm.

NORM Hey, Kev. What's the matter with you? You haven't said two words since we got on coach.

KEV Nowt, Norm. Just having a think.

NORM Push up, I'll sit next to you.

KEV Naw, I'm saving this one for Madelaine.

NORM Oh aye!

KEV Nowt like that. Just go through our lines a couple of times, make sure we got them right.

NORM Well – you're at the side of the stage, aren't you? Why not read them – you can't be seen, can you?

KEV Use your head, Norm, pitch black off stage, isn't it?

NORM Never thought of that. Hope I can see me props all right,

KEV Don't worry – Fred's bound to hover inconspicuously. He did the props during the heats – knows it backwards.

NORM Oh yeah – that's a thought. Here – budge up. I'll move out when we get to Loftborough, all right?

KEV Right.

Kev moves over and Norm sits down.

NORM That's better. Here – you know that thing that Eddie's up to, parent hunting. Well, I mentioned it to me mam – fishing like...

KEV He said not to say owt.

NORM I didn't say owt – I mean I didn't say what he was up to – I just said dead nonchalant, "Hey, I reckon if we knew who Little Eddie's real Mam and dad were, we'd know why he was so daft." And she went mad. Really tore into me. "You leave well alone," she said. "And mind your own business. Don't go stirring that up again after all these years." I was staggered.

KEV Funny – probably explains what my mam said. Yours must have told her – thick as thieves the both of them. She said, "Keep your eye on Little Eddie, see he doesn't get into any trouble." And I mean she knows he's not a special mate of mine or owt. If she'd said, "Keep your eye on daft Norm", I'd have understood.

NORM Hey! Watch it.

KEV You know what I mean.

NORM Could have put it a bit better. Still – seems a bit funny. Reckon the grown-ups know summat we don't?

KEV Yeah. Good isn't it? Bit like a mystery.

Fade for passage of time. Coach ticking over. The girls pour into the bus.

GUV (*distant*) Come on, girls. Hurry it up. London calls . . . Hello, Ethel . . .

There is a general exchange of greetings.

KEV (*close*) Up here, Mad.

MADELAINE Oh, hello Kev.

KEV I've kept you a seat.

MADELAINE Thanks, Kev. Needn't stand up.

KEV Thought you'd like to be near the window.

MADELAINE Oh, ta. Could've shoved past.

Settling down noises.

GUV Right! That it, Ethel?

ETHEL (*calling*) That's it, Guv.

GUV Okay, driver, off we go again. Next stop London.

The coach starts up. A general noise which fades under the following . . .

KEV What did your mam say about it, Mad?

MADELAINE I finally couldn't pluck up the courage to tell her.

KEV Oh.

MADELAINE Thought I'd wait till we'd looked round a few tomorrow. Get some prospectuses, that sort of thing – so I've more idea of the cost.

KEV The cost doesn't matter if you get a grant.

MADELAINE I know that but – I'm still not sure I'd be good enough, Kev.

KEV Course you would. Terrific. Bret said you're good, and that's big praise from him. Anyway – what does it matter? Get you away from Loftborough for a bit. Three years at least.

MADELAINE Loftborough's not that bad.

KEV Grangebank is.

MADELAINE Bet you'd miss your mates.

KEV Ah well – can't have everything.

MADELAINE Did you tell your mam?

KEV Aye. Went spare for a bit. Think she's all right about it now.

MADELAINE Didn't want to lose you?

KEV Naw. It's not an apron-string job – thinks I should finish me trade first.

MADELAINE Well – she might be right at that – come in handy when there's no acting around.

KEV Well – let's leave it for now. We'll see how it looks tomorrow.

MADELAINE Okay. You want to throw me a line?

KEV What?

MADELAINE Voices off – remember?

KEV Oh yes! Sunday – first time I'll have had you alone in the dark, and I'll have a mouthful of words.

MADELAINE (*mock tough guy*) Watch it, Grangebank Kev – else I'll get Ethel and the Loftborough girls on you.

KEV Oh no! A fate worse than Little Eddie!

10 The hotel foyer

Everybody is talking at once.

FRED (*above the hubbub*) Let's get them booked in quick, Ethel. Else it'll cost the hotel a fortune in lost trade.

ETHEL Right, Fred. (*Loudly*) Keep it down, girls! It's very late.

BRET All right, lads! Same goes for you!

Ad libbed "Okay Bret" etc. The background fades as we focus on Guv and Eddie.

GUV You do realise of course, Eddie, Ethel will never speak to me again – she's bound to think I put you up to it.

EDDIE 'Course she'll speak to you again, Guv. Anyway, she couldn't expect me to tell a lie now, could she – and she did ask me – she knows you always insist on the truth in our club – should do the same at Loftborough.

GUV There's two sorts of truth in this world, Eddie. True truth and diplomatic truth – if someone says "Have I got a big nose?" when they've got a big nose we don't say " 'Course you have, big nose" we use diplomatic truth, right?

EDDIE It wasn't her nose that we were talking about.

GUV I know that. But you could...

VI (*calling*) Eddie!

EDDIE Oh. Saved by the yell. Me Aunty Vi, Guv.

VI Eddie! So nice to see you again.

She cuddles him.

EDDIE Good. This is me Aunt Vi I told you about. This is...

VI Recognise him anywhere. Hello, Guv. Good to see you again.

GUV Oh, I'm sorry. Didn't know we'd...

VI Lot of years now. Your daughter Rose. Remember her friend, Violet?

GUV Violet! Well I never did, after all these years, little Violet – you haven't changed a bit...

EDDIE That's a diplomatic one, is it, Guv?

GUV ...so nice to see you again – I didn't realise. I hope we have chance to chat over the weekend.

VI Bound to. I'll be in and out, dropping Eddie off for rehearsals and things, and now his mam's written and told me how important Eddie's been to the success of the show so far...

EDDIE (*quickly*) Well, we'd better be off Aunt Vi, Guv's got to get the other kids sorted out and off to bed and things. Very busy. All right, Guv. Tara – see you in the theatre tomorrow.

11 The breakfast room

General clatter.

BRET Delicious.

FRED You can say that again, Bret.

BRET Right, Fred. Delicious.

GUV How'd you sleep, Bret?

BRET Terrible.

ETHEL I'm not surprised. You must have spent seven hours flat out and mouth open on the coach last evening.

BRET Usually doesn't make any difference – competition nerves, I think.

FRED Well – get the run through over today – finals tomorrow – into the coach – and have a nice sleep on the way home to make up the loss.

General laughter.

GUV Well, glancing around the assembled mass, I'd say all ours are accounted for – right, Fred?

FRED Right, Guv.

ETHEL Mine too. And I know they're all alright because they've been phoning me on the internal telephone since seven o'clock this morning to tell me so.

GUV You had that as well, did you? You'd think they were checking on us – seeing as how we decided not to check on them.

FRED No – a phone by the bed's irresistible. Free calls as well. I nearly phoned you all myself.

BRET Would have been nice to hear your cheery voice, Fred.

GUV What's your plans for today, Ethel?

ETHEL Museums – them that want to.

GUV Same with me and Fred this morning – then off to rehearsals. Bret?

BRET I'll go straight to the theatre, I think – stay there all day and keep an eye on our competitors.

FRED No sightseeing?

BRET No. I reckon once you've seen one Piccadilly Circus you've seen them all.

ETHEL But there only is one Piccadilly Circus, Bret.

BRET Proves me point, you see.

12 The theatre

BRET Okay, okay! Stop it there. Now look, it's dead on its feet. What's the matter with you all? You've never done it so badly. This is our last chance to have a go on stage before tomorrow and I've seen what you're up against, and I tell you now, if you all can't do better than this – get a bit of life into it, we've had it...
His voice fades under the following...

NORM It's at moments like this I'm glad I'm at the side of the stage, not on it. What do you say, Kev?

KEV (*very down*) Yup.

NORM Madelaine?

MADELAINE (*very down*) Yup.

NORM Eddie?

EDDIE (*very down*) Yup.

NORM Well – that was a sparkling bit of conversation. Do I take it your various bits of London business didn't go quite as well as planned – Kev?

KEV Yup.

NORM Madelaine?

MADELAINE Yup.

NORM Eddie?

EDDIE Yup.

NORM Ah well. There we are. I had a lovely time with Guv and Fred – Changing of the Guard. Buckingham Palace. National Gallery. Trafalgar Square...

EDDIE Norm?

NORM ... Piccadilly Circus... Cruise up the Thames.

EDDIE Norm.

NORM Yes, Eddie?

EDDIE I think Bret might suggest you keep your voice down in a minute if you go on like this.

BRET (*distant – but calling loudly*) Shut that noise up off stage, I'm trying to run a rehearsal!

EDDIE See what I mean?

13 The hotel lounge

GUV Eddie! What a nice surprise. Never expected to find you here crunched up in the corner of our posh hotel – what you up to, going out with the lads?

EDDIE (*very down*) No – waiting for me Aunt Vi. Hope you don't mind me waiting in here, Guv. Finished a bit early.

GUV 'Course not – want to come and have a cup of tea and a bit of cake while you're waiting?

EDDIE Naw. Said I'd hang on here. Better hang on.

GUV No panic – I'll pay for it.

EDDIE No thanks, Guv.

GUV Turning down free tea and cake! What's the world coming to? Not sickening for something are you, Eddie?

EDDIE Naw. Don't fancy it, that's all.

GUV (*pause as he sits*) Spit it out, Ed. What's the matter?

EDDIE (*pause*) Had a bit of business to attend to. Hasn't turned out too well, that's all.

GUV Want to tell me about it, get if off your chest like?

EDDIE Nowt to tell really. I had some places to go to. Everywhere I went was closed. Saturday. Dead funny really. "Can't tell you owt, mate – we work a five day week here. Anyway I'm only the porter, come back on Monday." Dead funny. Only wish I could laugh about it. Don't feel much like laughing today.

GUV Sure I can't help?

EDDIE Naw. I'm going to have a chat with me Aunt Vi tonight – see if she can help.

GUV Okay. But – you know I'm here if there's any problems. All right?

EDDIE All right, Guv.

14 Near the river

Footsteps walking slowly along. A tugboat hoots.

MADELAINE Isn't it lovely along here?

KEV Aye. It's a pretty river all right. Hundreds of lights everywhere – almost nice enough to jump in.

MADELAINE Oh come on, Kev – it's not that bad.

KEV Well – I can't work people out, I really can't, Mad. I mean we were only being civil and it seemed nobody had two seconds to spare.

MADELAINE Well that's what London's like it seems – I haven't seen anyone outside our lot smile since we got here.

KEV I didn't want 'em to smile, Mad. Just be civil, that's all. I mean it was simple. "What's it like here, mate?" and "Where do we get forms from to join?" – always the same "No time to talk, come back next week", "Write in". Nobody interested even – looking at us as if we were idiots or country yokels or something.

MADELAINE Well – I suppose when you think about it if somebody turned up out the blue on Saturday morning when you were working and said, "What's it like here, mate?", "Where do we get a form to join?" they'd probably seem a bit strange to you.

KEV Suppose you're right.
Big Ben strikes the half hour.
Better get back to the hotel. Nearly curfew time. Don't want to get Guv and Ethel worried.

15 The hotel

A lift door opens. "Goodnights" being called to Guv.

ETHEL Don't stay up chatting too long the pair of you.

GUV That goes for you as well, Kev.

KEV Right, Guv. Goodnight.

MADELAINE Okay, Ethel. Goodnight all.
They go.

GUV Well, that's the last of mine, Ethel.

ETHEL And mine. I think I'll be off up myself. Long day tomorrow. Goodnight all.

FRED Me too. Goodnight, Guv, Bret.

GUV Goodnight, Ethel, Fred.

BRET Goodnight.

Ethel and Fred go.

Like a nightcap, Guv?

GUV No thanks, Bret.

BRET No, don't think I'll bother either.

GUV (*pause*) What do you think, Bret?

BRET Our chances?

GUV Yes.

BRET Well, being honest – on today's performance, no way. But there again – it's often that way at last rehearsals so you can't really tell. Mind you there's some really stiff competition there.

GUV Anyone special?

BRET Well, the Leeds club's the really exceptional one. Knockout – still we'll wait and see. Anyway, it's not really about winning, is it? They've all had their first trip to London – nice couple of days. Winning's very secondary, wouldn't you say?

GUV Who you trying to kid, Bret – not me I hope?

BRET No – myself I think. Right – I'm off up.

GUV Aye me too. Hope you manage to get some sleep tonight.

BRET And you.

GUV No problem. My head touches the pillow I'm out like a light.

16 Hotel bedroom

Gentle snoring. The telephone rings piercingly.

GUV (*to himself*) What! Where . . . oh . . . time is it? . . . One thirty-five . . . If that's someone messing about I'll have them shredded . . . Bedside light on – see what I'm doing . . . (*Click*) . . . There we are.

He picks up the phone.
... If that's you, Bret, it's not funny... Yes – that's me speaking. Yes... Is she on the phone like?... In reception!... Bit upset you say... right... I'm on my way down... Can you fix her up with a cup of tea or something... good lad. I'll be there in two ticks.
He puts the phone down.

17 The hotel foyer

The lift doors open and Guv comes in.

GUV (*enquiringly*) Porter?

PORTER I put her through in the residents' lounge, sir – quiet in there.

GUV Right. I'll go through. That tea coming, is it?

PORTER Yes, sir.

Gentle crying grows nearer as we approach.

GUV Violet?

VI Oh, Guv. Something terrible's happened – all my fault.

GUV Little Eddie?

VI Yes.

GUV He's not hurt, is he?

VI Yes – very hurt. But not the way you mean. All my fault as well. He's gone, Guv.

GUV What do you mean, gone?

VI Gone – run away.

GUV Run away? Little Eddie?

VI Tonight. About half past eleven – he ran out of the house. He didn't come back so after about half an hour I went off searching up and down every street in the area. Couldn't find him anywhere. He's gone, Guv.

GUV What on earth possessed him to do owt so daft as run off?

VI (*pause*) I... He... Oh, Guv. (*She cries*)

GUV (*comforting*) There, there. Come on now, Vi. Remember you're a Grangebank lass at heart. Not as bad as all that. If it's Eddie's going lost that worries you – forget it. Anyone who can survive fifteen and a half years of Vaughan Street is going to have no problem sorting London out.

VI He's got nowhere else to go.

GUV I always teach my lads to go off to the local police station in an emergency – if they're stuck for somewhere to sleep or owt. He'll be all right, Vi – you'll see. He'll be back right as rain tomorrow. I'm a bit worried about the police, mind. They're only used to ordinary villains down here. Not someone subtle like Eddie.

VI Oh, Guv.

GUV Come on, Vi. Spit it out. Something about the bit of business he kept saying he had to do down here, was it?

VI Yes.

GUV What was he up to? He didn't say – can you tell me?

VI He was trying to find out who his real parents were.

GUV Ah, the silly tyke. Why didn't he check with me? This business about orphaned kids finding out their real parents has gone to all their heads. Got to be eighteen at least before they'll consider it even. Counselling to go through, all sorts of things. Not a weekend job at all.

VI It wasn't that. That wasn't what got him thinking. That Kevin's dad dying was what started it. He said, "If you don't know who they are, where they live, how can you know when they die?" You know how he talks, Guv. "I could be eating a bag of crisps, having a half pint with me mates and a bit of a giggle; and my old man could be snuffing it. Wouldn't be right, Aunt Vi. Wouldn't be right, would it?"

GUV (*pause*) Certainly wouldn't. Two and a half years by my reckoning before he can go in a pub for a drink. Anyway what the lump doesn't realise is there's no way he can find out in any case – he's a foundling not an orphan. I suppose that's what you told him that upset him so much, was it, Vi?

VI No – that's not what I told him. (*Long pause*) I told him his mother was no good. Not worth bothering with. Anyone who deserts someone as nice as him doesn't deserve to be remembered – doesn't deserve to be loved. Better off dead – in his mind if not in fact – forget her, she's worthless.

GUV (*angry*) That's a bloody stupid thing to say, you should have more sense. You know the sort of kid he is. How dare you decide that someone he doesn't know, but loves, should be dead. What right have you to say anything so hurtful to one of my boys?

VI (*long pause*) The greatest right in the world. (*pause*) I'm his mother.

GUV (*long pause*) Good God!

18 Kev's room

MADELAINE Well, I'd better get back to my room, Kev – it's getting a bit late.

KEV Aye. It's been really nice talking to you, Mad.

MADELAINE And to you.

KEV Mad...

MADELAINE Yes, Kev.

KEV ... If you really mean you're not going to try for this Drama course thing...

MADELAINE Don't think I can, Kev. Having seen the places I've lost my nerve completely.

KEV ... Well, supposing I put off going for a couple of years like...

MADELAINE But you really want to go.

KEV ... I know but... I could finish me time, cheer me mam up like, and you said yourself a trade's handy to fall back on when there's no acting around.

MADELAINE I know but...

KEV The real reason is – what I'm trying to say is... I don't really want to be down here, if you're up there, if you see what I mean. (*Pause*) What

I'm really trying to say is ... I'd like to be your bloke.

MADELAINE Oh.

KEV I know we tried a few years back, but I didn't have a bike so I couldn't get over to Loftborough and nowt came of it. Well, I've got me motorbike now, so that's no problem anymore – what do you say, Mad?

MADELAINE (*pause*) I say it'd be lovely. Let's seal the deal before you change your mind.

KEV Sounds good.

They kiss. A knock on the door.

MADELAINE (*whispers*) Ethel!

KEV (*whispers*) Guv!

Knock, knock on the door. Spoken "Knock, Knock".

KEV Who's there?

EDDIE "Freda".

KEV (*bemused*) Freda? (*Calls*) Freda who?

EDDIE "Freda can't tell you till you open the door".

KEV I don't believe it.

He crosses to the door and opens it.

Eddie!

EDDIE Hello, Kev. Oh – hello, Madelaine. Shall we have a line practice now we're all together?

KEV What the hell you up to, Eddie?

EDDIE You know you said if I needed your help to tell you.

KEV Yes.

EDDIE Well, I need your help.

KEV You're joking – it's gone half past one.

EDDIE I know – and I want to go to bed – and I haven't got a bed to go to – so I want a share of yours.

MADELAINE I'd better be off.

KEV Hang on, Mad.

EDDIE Sorry to interrupt. Didn't mean to. I'll go over there and sit and look out the window if you like until ...

KEV There's nowt like that going on, we're just chatting.

EDDIE Oh.

MADELAINE I better be off, Kev. Early start tomorrow.

KEV Okay, Mad. See you tomorrow. You won't forget our deal?

MADELAINE No way. 'Night, Ed. 'Night, Kev. See you at the side of the stage.

KEV 'Night, Mad.

EDDIE 'Night, Madelaine.

She goes closing the door behind her.

You do realise you're scowling at me, Kevin. (*Pause*) Do you want your head at the top of the bed, or the bottom of the bed? (*Pause*) Both better wash our feet, had we?

KEV What happened?

EDDIE Had a few words, that's all. Thought it best to leave. Came here. Been wandering round for half an hour knocking on doors looking for you or Norm.

KEV You haven't?

EDDIE I have. Didn't like to ask downstairs case I got kicked out. Bret wasn't terribly pleased when I woke him up.

KEV But why? Why did you leave your Aunt Vi's?

EDDIE She said something that wasn't very nice about me real mam.

KEV She knew who it was then?

EDDIE Naw – no idea. Just general things. I suppose it was my fault really. I got off on the wrong foot with a bit of a bad joke about your dad.

KEV My dad? What bad joke?

EDDIE Well – you might get a bit bad tempered, so can we sort out whether I can stay, and which end of the bed I'm at, first, Kev?

KEV 'Course you can stay – but I'm at the top and don't try to con it off me.

EDDIE Okay.

KEV Right – what bad joke?

EDDIE Well – I was trying to explain how your dad dying got me thinking about it, and it's a long time since she's lived up there, and I was explaining who he is – you know describing him like, always drunk and whistling and happy and that . . .

KEV Oh thank you very much.

EDDIE ...You know what I mean. Anyway she finally twigged who I was talking about, before I told her he'd died like, and she said "Oh, yes of course, 'Whistling Wally' – always whistling, isn't he?" And I said "He doesn't whistle any more now." And I know it's very wrong, Kev, but when she said a bit posh – "Hasn't he got the breath for it anymore?" I said, "No. He hasn't got the breath for owt – he's snuffed it."

KEV (*pause*) Not much of a joke.

EDDIE No. Don't suppose it was really. Funny thing was but, it was if I'd slapped her. Her whole face sort of crumpled. And you won't believe this, Kev – but she started to cry. Tears and everything.

19 Back in the lounge

VI You know what Grangebank's like. Be a big enough scandal now so you imagine what it would have been like fifteen years ago. My brother was very good about it. Arranged for me to go away to have it at other relatives so no one knew. Him and Marge couldn't have kids – seemed sensible they should adopt but they were a bit old – so it was planned that they'd find him and keep him. Two days after it was born we met at their house when it was dark. Then I went ahead, they followed behind – and I put the bag down in the Bottom House doorway, seconds later they picked it up, making a lot of fuss attracting the people in the pub, so everyone knew they'd found it there. (*Pause*) I went off and got the train to London. Started a new life.

GUV Why have you never told Eddie? He's old enough to understand now, for all his daft tricks.

VI I've got a nice husband and two nice kids, Guv. How do you tell a husband you had a baby when you were sixteen, that he knows nowt about?

GUV Well, Eddie's going to find out sometime. He'll get hold of the birth certificate or get a copy or summat – what happens then?

VI He gets a bit of a surprise. *I* didn't register him. And my brother knew if they took the baby to the proper authorities, chances are they wouldn't be allowed to keep him. If Eddie gets hold of his birth certificate he finds out what every adult in Vaughan Street knows, and has kept quiet about all these years. He finds out that the mam and dad who've brought him up, and made no secret of the fact that he's a foundling, are registered on the birth certificate, as his real mam and dad.

20 The bedroom

Eddie is crying quietly. Kev wakes.

KEV (*sleepy*) Ed.

EDDIE (*stops crying, gets control*) What?

KEV What's the matter?

EDDIE Nowt.

KEV Did I put my toe in your eye or summat?

EDDIE No.

KEV What's the matter then?

EDDIE (*pause*) I'll never know when they die, Kev.

KEV Don't get back to that again, Ed. Getting a bit boring. It's no good worrying now. Anyway, it's not that special knowing they're dead.

EDDIE I'll never dare laugh again.

KEV You're being daft about it. My Uncle Joe had it weighed up. Though I didn't believe him at the time. People dying's like packing up smoking he said. First it hurts like hell and you think you'll never manage to get over the hurt, but before you know it the first really bad days are over; and within weeks you go minutes, then hours, then days, without even remembering, might even feel bad about it, but you still get twinges to remind you now and again– and you know you'll never be completely cured, but you can live with it – see what I mean?

EDDIE Aye – but until I find out what bloody brand I smoke I can't pack up, can I?

KEV (*pause*) Aye – suppose you're right.

Kev sits up sharply in bed.

Eddie!

EDDIE What?

KEV I've got it! Dead simple. I know the answer!

21 The lounge of the hotel

GUV (*softly*) How about the father?

VI (*pause*) He never knew. Never told him. And I never told anyone who he was. Not even my brother.

GUV (*long pause*) Want to get it off your chest, Vi? You know it'll be safe with me – might be nice if someone knows. Case owt happens. For Eddie's sake more than anything.

Long pause.

VI Like a dream really. Lovely summer night. He knew I liked him. I didn't have to say. He knew all right. That night I was at the corner of the street. He was out of work, didn't have the price of a pint even. Said he was going for a walk up the hills. Would I like to come? The number of times I'd dreamed that might happen. Even though he was married and had kids, it didn't matter. We laughed so much on the way. It was lovely. I'd never been so happy. And finally, we sat at the top of Eston Hills and looked down at the works, all the lights twinkling through the smoke. He pointed out different places he'd worked, seemed as though he'd worked everywhere. And he told me his dreams. Daft really. I knew they'd never come true, couldn't come true. But he shared them. Then he stood. High above the works. Stood, sort of defiant.

As she remembers the past, we hear the sound of the wind soughing over a high hillside. Unaccompanied whistling cutting through the sound. Hold under the following.

He whistled. A tune I'd heard him whistle so many times before; when I was a kid – as he went home drunk; as I grew towards being a woman, always the same tune. A tune fit to melt the heart of a street. Make it forget how mean and dirty it was. A tune that made it impossible for me to say no when he asked me. Even if I'd wanted to, which I didn't. There on the hills, high above Grangebank. He asked me – I said yes. For the first and only time – we made love.

The sounds die away.

Sorry. Almost forgot you were here, Guv. (*Pause*) You know?

GUV (*long pause*) I know.

22 The theatre after the performance

LONDON ADJUDICATOR ... and I have no hesitation at all in placing them into a very well deserved third position.

Clapping loud and sustained.

And now – the result of the closest run battle I personally have ever seen in over fifteen years of adjudicating, and the first time I've been tempted by the possibility of declaring joint winners. I fought the temptation and declare, a mere whisker away from the top, that second place goes to Leeds Boys' and Girls' Club!

Clapping, cheers; one or two "We was robbed".

And so now to the winners of this year's National Association of Boys' and Girls' Clubs Drama finals. The other side of that whisker, and I must say publicly, that the quality of the unseen actors who provided such a wide variety of voices offstage, tipped the balance in their favour. Ladies and gentlemen, in first place – Grangebank Boys' Club!

Tumultuous cheering. Kev, Mad, Norm's ad libbed comments added. Clapping, cheering ad libs.

23 Outside the hotel

The coach engine ticking over. People getting in.

FRED All aboard!

GUV How we doing, Fred?

FRED Filling up nicely, Guv. Where's Eddie?

GUV He's in the lounge saying his goodbyes to Vi. No panic. Recalcitrance behind him.

FRED Pardon?

GUV No more running off for our Eddie, I don't think.

FRED Good job for you he knocked on Bret's door last night and Bret managed finally to find you.

GUV You can say that again. There was me trying to comfort Vi – while desperately wondering how I could get to a phone and get the police out looking for our little lost in London. Bret's news that Eddie was wandering round the hotel was a great relief all right.

FRED Aye. I bet. What was it all about, Guv?

GUV Well – long story, Fred. Best not get into it.

FRED Fair enough. Someday?

GUV Aye. Like as not. But a long time yet, Fred. A long time yet.

24 The hotel lounge

EDDIE Well – better get off then.

VI Aye. Well. Congratulations again, Eddie – glad your lot won. They were very good. Really really good. You too.

EDDIE Yeah. (*Pause*) Look, Aunt Vi, I'm sorry I ran off and frightened you like that last night.

VI That's all right, Eddie. No harm done, it's over now. Forgotten. You're safe, that's all that matters.

EDDIE Not quite. There's a few other things that matter too. Aunty. For a start I think you were wrong.

VI Wrong?

EDDIE To say what you said. (*Pause*) You see it's funny really – if any of the blokes said owt nasty about me real mam – I'd hit them, even though I'm quite small. Even though I don't know who she is – because she's me real mam. You said something nasty, but I couldn't hit you, you're a woman, you're me Aunt Vi. So I ran away. But I've thought about it, about what you said. And I think you're wrong. (*Pause*) Whoever she is, wherever she is, I think she had her reasons for doing what she did. I don't think she was a tart like you suggested. And even if she was I wouldn't give a damn – she's me mam. Me real mam. And you shouldn't say bad things about her. And another funny thing is Aunt Vi – I'm not worried about *her* being dead – because I know she's not, you know why? 'Cos none of me mates' mams have died yet – and I'm never first at owt. A good second maybe, but never first; so she's alive somewhere. And she'll never know I love her. But I do. And that's what matters.

VI (*long pause*) And your dad? The same applies?

EDDIE (*pause*) Too late. He's dead. I found out last night. Too hard to explain. 'Bye, Vi. See you again sometime. I'll tell mam what a lovely time I had. 'Bye.

Eddie goes out through the foyer and gets on the coach. The doors slide shut.

GUV All right, driver. That's your lot, we're off.

The coach drives off.

FRED Well, there we are, Guv.

GUV There we are, Fred. Crossword?

FRED Aye, why not. Easy one to give ourselves a treat?

GUV Fair enough.

Looking through the crossword.

FRED Here we are. One across. Voice like an angel. Five letters beginning with . . .

Voice close and loud: "We won the cup, we won the cup."

GUV Speak of the devil, Fred.

Guv half stands to look behind.

GUV Hello, Eddie! What a pleasant surprise. How many letters in your name by the way?

EDDIE Hello, Guv. Six, why?

GUV Six?

EDDIE Yes, Edward. Six letters.

GUV Edward! Are you called Edward?

EDDIE Yeah.

GUV What a silly name. Why are you bawling in my ear, Edward, instead of Ethel's ear? Haven't you done enough damage for one weekend?

EDDIE Shouldn't have told her the 'Buffer' secret should I? She made straight for the back seat when she got on so I couldn't get behind her.

GUV What a rotten trick.

EDDIE Yeah. Can't trust women, can you? Didn't like to say owt but. So I decided to make the best of a bad job and get behind you.

GUV I'll soon foil that. Excuse me, Fred. I'm off for a chat with our Edward.

FRED Right. I'll keep the hard ones for you.

Guv changes seats.

GUV Budge up, Ed.

EDDIE Right, Guv. Great winning, wasn't it?

GUV Yes – but it's not everything, Ed. Don't forget that.

EDDIE Who you trying to kid, guv?

GUV Not really everything – but quite nice.

EDDIE Well – I've really won out this weekend. Went away an orphan and came back with a dad – great.

GUV (*pause, then carefully*) What do you mean, Ed?

EDDIE Kev's idea really. See he twigged the problem with me is not *not* having a dad, but – not knowing when he dies, right? It's hard to explain really, but Kev worked it out – and to make it all alright, he sort of adopted me as a brother like. I mean he nearly jumped out of bed when the idea struck him.

GUV What exactly did Kev do, Eddie?

EDDIE Well, he gave me a dad and bumped him off all the same time you see. So simple it's brilliant.

GUV You've lost me.

EDDIE Look – Kev said, "Share my dad – if you like" and I said, "What use is that, he's dead already" and he said, "Well – all the better, isn't it? You know what's happened to him – you know how he died, you know what sort of bloke he was. We can both have a good cry and get it over with." (*Pause*) See? (*Pause*) You'll laugh, Guv. You'll really laugh when I tell you, but there I was at one end of the bed, with Kev's toes near enough stuck up me nose, and there was Kev at the other end, with my toes near enough stuck up his nose – and you'll never believe it, Guv – but we both cried our bloody eyes out. (*Pause*) You all right, Guv? You look a bit funny.

GUV (*long pause*) Yes – fine, Eddie. Fine. Bit of a turn. You go back to "We won the cup", all right?

EDDIE Right.

GUV I'll go back and aggravate Fred.

Guv settles back in his seat. Slightly distant, Eddie sings.

FRED (*worried*) You all right, Guv? Look a bit – ghost treading on grave – ish.

GUV It's all right, Fred. I'm fine. Just been struck by a thought. When life's at its funniest – playing the biggest jokes – that's the time when one realises the balance between laughter and tears is a very fine balance indeed. A very fine balance indeed, Fred.

The sound of the group singing "We won the cup" rises to a crescendo before dying away.

Little Weed's Big Day

Chris Curry

The Cast

Jem Clegg

Ben Parker

Cheyenne

Lightnin'

Joe Clog

Raptash

Collie

A man

Grandma

Little Weed's Big Day

1 A street (morning)

JEM (*groaning and puffing*) Oh, no. Come on, Esmerelda. Don't let's be having one of your funny do's. Come on... (*Sighing*) ...ay, I can't make you out... I can't...every other morning you start like a little good-un for me... (*He strains*)...but... Mondays it's always the same...

BEN (*diffidently*) Mr Clegg?

JEM (*hasn't heard and is still struggling*) We'll be late if you don't... Oh, come *on*...

BEN (*slightly louder*) Er... Mr Clegg?

Esmerelda's engine suddenly bursts into life.

JEM (*chuckling gleefully*) You little belter... I knew you could do it... you little belter...

BEN Mr Clegg, me Dad said...

JEM (*becoming aware of his visitor for the first time*) Hello, lad, and what can we be doing for you? Wanting a lift to school?

BEN (*thrown by this deviation from his rehearsed speech*) Oh, no... I... no... I've left school, Mr Clegg... and me Dad said...

JEM Oh, aye. Learnt it all, have you?

BEN Yes... no... er... me Dad said...

JEM He has a lot to say for himself, your Dad, hasn't he?

BEN Yes... no... well, he just said...

JEM Jacky Parker's young-un, aren't you? Mayberry Street?

BEN Yes, Mr Clegg.

JEM Aye. Benjamin, is it?

BEN Yes, Mr Clegg and me Dad said...

JEM Aye, I remember... Nearly ran you over when you were a nipper. Four or five you'd be... (*He winces*) played merry-hell with me, your Mam... said she'd fetch the Bobbies...

BEN (*proud to be remembered*) I know, she told me. (*The memory more painful now*) Me Dad didn't half paste me – said I shouldn't have been playing in the middle of the street...

JEM No more you should. (*Short pause*) So! You've finished wi' schooling then?

BEN Yes, Mr Clegg.

JEM And your Dad said, "Go and ask Jem Clegg if he can do owt with you"?

BEN Yes, Mr Clegg.

JEM (*considering the applicant*) Mmm. Have you finished growing, do you reckon?

BEN (*self-consciously*) I don't know, Mr Clegg... me Dad says...

JEM Smoke, do you?

BEN No, Mr Clegg!

JEM That'll stunt your growth, you know. You want to remember that...

BEN I know, Mr Clegg, me Dad told me...

JEM (*still considering*) Mmm. Well...

He lights up a cigarette.

You're not so big...

BEN Me Mam said it were daft, me Dad sending to you. Me Mam said I was too little...

JEM You tell your Mam from me being big's nowt to do with it.

BEN Yes, Mr Clegg.

JEM (*pause*) Well! Are you coming or what?

BEN You what, Mr Clegg?

JEM Well, if you're coming, you'd best be getting a move on. We've three ton of coal to shift on and off this lorry before tea-time...

BEN Do you mean...? Come with you? Now like?

JEM Well we'll never make a coal-bagger out of you standing there, will we?

BEN (*excited*) No, Mr Clegg.

JEM Jump in the cab then!

BEN Yeah! Right! Right, Mr Clegg...

He jumps in and bangs the door shut. The lorry starts to move off.

... And ... thanks, Mr Clegg.

JEM Aye, well, you'll happen not be thanking me tonight, Benjamin Parker – if you ever get that far ... (*He laughs*) I've known 'em be carried off on a stretcher before dinner time ...

BEN *I'll* not, Mr Clegg! Honest! I'll not!

JEM (*laughing*) Aye, well. We'll see, lad. We'll see ...

The engine fades into the distance.

2 The yard

Men are talking and laughing in the hut which constitutes the yard office.

CHEYENNE (*seemingly choking*) Here! Lightnin'! Have you washed your long-combs out in that there teapot of yours or what?

LIGHTNIN' (*speaking excruciatingly slowly and prefacing every statement with a long, sighing 'aaay'*) Aaay, I don't know what you want, you lot. It's not the bloody Park Café, you know ...

CHEYENNE You're not kidding.

JOE CLOG Hey, Lightnin'! You ever thought of using *tea* to make it with – 'stead of anthracite? Be a bloody sight cheaper ...

LIGHTNIN' Aaay, I don't know. Anyway, you shouldn't be sitting in here by rights, you know, Joe Clog. It's not the bloody-Park-Cafe' ...

CHEYENNE Here! Shut up and pour us another mugful of that ... maiden's water. (*Short pause*) Jem's leaving it late this morning, in't he? Usually first here ...

JOE CLOG Be that wagon of his – playing him up. Time he got rid. Mind you, there's only t'British Museum'd take it off his hands. By heck, though, Cheyenne, have you seen them new uns? Like Rolls Royces they are – radios – that there – air conditioning ... reclining seats ...

CHEYENNE Sounds better than our house.

Door opens and in comes Jem followed by Ben.

JEM Now then, Cheyenne. Joe.

CHEYENNE Mornin', Jem. Esmerelda been giving you bother?

JEM No. Started first time. Always does.

CHEYENNE Oh, aye. 'Bout had it if you ask me, Jem. Time you got yourself one of them new uns...

JEM Aye, well. Plenty of time to think of changing when she lets me down. Any tea going, Lightnin'?

LIGHTNIN' Aaay. You're only supposed to come in here to sign your loads out, you lot, you know... It's against the coal company's regulations to...

JEM And give us a mug for the lad here while you're at it...

LIGHTNIN' Aaay, anybody'd think it were t'bloody Park...

CHEYENNE Now then. Who's this you've got with you, Jem? It looks like it belongs in t'girls' school. What they call you, young-un?

BEN (*very quietly*) Er... Ben.

JEM Jacky Parker's lad. You know? Mayberry Street. (*Chokes on the tea*) Ugh! How long you had *this* in the pot, Lightnin'?

LIGHTNIN' (*muttering to himself*) Aaay, shouldn't be in here by rights...

JOE CLOG Parker. Parker. Aye! I know him. Big fella i'n't he, your Dad? Played a bit for the team, didn't he?

BEN Yeah, he did.

JOE CLOG Aye! I know him! Built like a corporation lav. What happened to you then?

BEN I don't know... er... I... me Dad says....

CHEYENNE (*laughing*) Happen their milkman was a bit on t' skinny side... hey, young-un?

JEM (*not amused*) There's no call for that sort of talk, Cheyenne, and you'd best not let his Dad catch you saying owt of the sort. You might be big but I reckon Jacky Parker'd knock you as far back as Boadicea with one good thump.

CHEYENNE (*teasing*) Naw, his Dad's past it, i'n't he, young-un?

BEN (*defending family honour*) He's not!

CHEYENNE Yea, it's all turned to fat – not got muscles like *these* any more, has he, young-un?

BEN (*as if his defence scares him more than it does his attacker*) He has... he has!

JEM Oh, leave the lad alone, Cheyenne... you're worse than a big soft kid at times...

CHEYENNE (*laughing*) Only having a laugh with him, Jem, aren't I . . . ? *What* is it they call you?

BEN Ben.

JOE CLOG Ben. Rum name. Oh, aye . . . (*He sings*) Bill and Ben, Bill and Ben . . . Flowerpot . . .

JEM And *you* can put a sock in it and all, Joe Clog. *You* weren't so much to look at yourself when you were his age . . .

JOE CLOG Nay, Jem, I'd a bit more meat on me than this young whippet . . .

JEM Not as I recall . . .

CHEYENNE (*laughing and singing*) Bill and Ben, Bill and Ben . . . Flowerpot . . . (*He laughs*) Hey, Joe, he looks more like that there Little Weed to me . . .

JOE CLOG (*laughing*) Aye. Aye. Little Weed.

CHEYENNE (*pleased with his joke*) Little Weed. Here! Lightnin', give Little Weed some more sugar in this tea! See if we can't build him up a bit, otherwise he'll get flattened under t'first bag of coal he hoists . . .

BEN Me Dad says you don't have to be strong . . . me Dad says it's a *knack* . . .

CHEYENNE Aye, it's a 'knack' all right. It's called bloody hard work. (*He laughs*)

JEM You weren't so clever yourself, Cheyenne, when you first started helping with me. Don't you go forgetting that. (*He laughs*) I can see you now – tipping *yourself* into t'bunker with the first bag you took . . .

CHEYENNE Ah, well, I was only a learner then, Jem . . .

JEM Aye, and you're still a learner as far as I'm concerned. To look at you then nobody'd have credited you ever having a round of your own . . .

CHEYENNE So! Little Weed! And it's your first job, is it?

BEN Er . . . yeah. I just left school.

CHEYENNE Big day for you then.

JOE CLOG Hey up! Look to your beds! Raptash is coming!

JEM Take your time, lad. No rush.

CHEYENNE Hey up, Lightnin'! Straighten your pinny – your boss's here.

The door opens.

RAPTASH (*coming in and shivering*) Good morning, gentlemen. Good morning. Quite a severe blast from the east this morning.

JEM (*flatly*) Aye, with a bit of luck we'll be knee-deep in snow by tomorrow.

BEN (*interested*) Do you *like* snow, Mr Clegg?

CHEYENNE (*mocking*) Do you like snow, Mr Clegg? (*He laughs*) Do you like snow? Well, you don't sell much bloody coal when the sun's cracking the flags, do you, you daft little...

LIGHTNIN' Will you be wanting tea, Mr Merrick?

RAPTASH No, thanking you kindly, Lightfoot. I have my thermos of coffee... as I normally...

LIGHTNIN' Aaay, I don't know how anybody can sup that stuff ...

CHEYENNE It can't be much worse than that 'orrible tea of yours, Lightnin'...

RAPTASH Of course, this office is not, strictly speaking, supposed to be *used* as a place for the serving of refreshments...

JOE CLOG (*laughing*) Well, you've only to taste Lightnin's tea and you'll know you've nowt to worry about *there*, Mr Merrick.

RAPTASH Strictly speaking, of course, this office is purely intended for the signing out of loads... It isn't, strictly speaking, ordained to be used as an unofficial social club...

JEM Oh, aye.

RAPTASH No, the Asherton Coal Company provides this office...

CHEYENNE Office! I've a better shed on my allotment!

RAPTASH ...provides this *office* as a service to the coal dealers and as a place where the loads can be signed for and...

JEM Well, I'll tell you what, Mr Merrick, you get sat down at that there adding machine of yours and let us know how much you're going to charge us for a pint of water each... Oh! and gas to boil it up with, and you can add it on to the bill at the end of the week... along with your coal...

JOE CLOG We buy the tea ourselves you know, Mr Merrick. Don't we, Lightnin'? Don't we give you the money for the tea?

LIGHTNIN' Aaay, don't go fetching me into it.

CHEYENNE Well, tell him, Lightnin'! Don't just stand there looking gormless... Mind, I don't suppose you can help your nature...

RAPTASH And then, of course, strictly speaking, there is Lightfoot's *time* to take into account...

JEM (*getting up*) Aye, well happen you can tot that up on your bill and all. Come on, Ben lad, this'll not shift any coal...

BEN (*eagerly*) Oh. Right! Right, Mr Clegg!

CHEYENNE (*getting up*) Aye, you're right, Jem, this'll not knit the babby a bonnet... And we can't go buying all this coal off of the Asherton Coal Company and not delivering it, can we?

RAPTASH Quite right, gentlemen. Tempus fugit. Tempus fugit indeed. We all have our work to do.

JEM Oh, aye.

They all go outside.

CHEYENNE Jcees, it's bloody freezing. Collie not turned up then, Jem?

JEM No, and I'll... 'fugit' him when he does. He were late two mornings last week.

JOE CLOG (*teasing*) Ah, you don't need Collie, Jem, when you've got Little Weed here! You can shift a ton before dinner time, *can't* you, Little Weed?

BEN I... er... I don't know.

JEM Well, it looks like you might have to, lad. 'Bye. I'll *murder* that Collie one of these...

CHEYENNE Anyway, Jem. Me and Joe'll get on our way. Get loaded up. We'll see you at dinner time... if you ever manage to get round with Little Weed here... (*As he walks away*) C'mon, Cloggy, let's make a start before me blood freezes...

JOE CLOG Aye, right! I'm fit, Cheyenne. Sooner we get started, sooner we get done.

CHEYENNE (*singing as he goes off*) St Peter, don't you call me, 'cause I can't goooo. I owe my soul to the company store...'

JEM (*blowing with the cold and then sighing*) Right, come on then, lad... It looks like it's just thee and me.

BEN Right, Mr Clegg. (*He sniffs*)

The hut door opens just as they start to walk away.

RAPTASH Mr Clegg ... er ... just one moment if you would!

JEM (*calling back*) Well, I'm a bit pushed, Mr Merrick ...

RAPTASH Well, if I could just have a word ... before you start to load ...

JEM Well, I've only the lad here, Mr Merrick, Collie's not turned in and ... I'll catch you at dinner time ...

RAPTASH Well, strictly speaking, Clegg, it oughtn't to wait ... We *are* a little concerned ...

JEM (*walking away*) Aye, right ... well, I'll be sure to catch you ... at dinner time ...
(*He has now left Ben behind*) Come on, lad! ... Or have you changed your mind? About being a coal-bagger?

BEN (*running after him*) No! No, Mr Clegg. I'm coming!

3 The back of Jem's wagon

Sacks being pushed around. Two pairs of boots sounding heavily on the wagon base.

JEM Come on, lad. Pass me another bag ...

BEN (*tugging*) I can't, Mr Clegg. I can't get it off the pile. They're frozen together ... solid ...

JEM Here, let's have a see ... (*He struggles and then gives up*) Aargh. See, run back to Lightnin' with this can ... Get him to fill it up with water for you ...

BEN Water, Mr Clegg?

JEM (*rather impatiently*) Aye. You know? Wet stuff. Comes down taps. (*Getting no confirmation of understanding from Ben*) To pour over the sacks! So we can get 'em apart

BEN Oh. But ... but they'll be all wet then, Mr Clegg.

JEM (*he really does seem to be losing patience*) Well, it's better than 'em being frozen bloody stiff, in'it!?

BEN Oh, yeah. Right! Right, Mr Clegg, I'll go and ...
Ben runs off with the can.

JEM (*calling after him*) And don't be all day! (*To himself now*) It'll be too bloody dark to deliver it at this rate ...
Footsteps – unhurried – approaching.

COLLIE Morning.

JEM (*doesn't stop working and is sullen in his reply*) Aye – it *were*.

COLLIE (*quite cheerfully stating a fact*) I'm a bit late.

JEM Aye.

COLLIE (*not daunted by the curt reply*) Eeh, you should have seen it down at the club last night, Jem . . .

JEM (*still sulking*) Happen be better if *you'd* seen a bit less of it . . . (*Muttering to himself*) . . . nearly bloody knocking-off time . . .

COLLIE (*chuckling as he recalls*) You've never seen a "do" like it. I'm not kidding, they'd a fella on – doing a turn like – "strong man" he called himself . . . great Nellie . . . Anyway, "I want two of you nice big strong fellas," he says. "I'm going to coil this rope around me neck and I want two of your biggest men to come and take hold of each end and pull as hard as they can. I can take all the strain you can muster," he says . . .

JEM (*as if he's not listening*) Pass that fifty-sixer over.

COLLIE Here y'are. Aye, aye, so me and Dylan goes up – volunteers like . . . (*He is hardly able to contain his laughter*) So, Dylan gives me the wink like and . . . Well, we knew what he were on – knew what the game were. He was going to give himself time to brace up . . . So! Dylan gives me the wink and, soon as he gets the rope draped round his neck, we both pull like hell . . . (*He laughs*) You've never seen owt like it . . . arms flapping about everywhere . . . wasn't ready you see . . . Trying to tell us to let go . . . purple he was. He's clawing at the rope and me and Dylan's smiling at him – pretending we thought we was doing it right – and pulling like hell and . . .

JEM Looks like he got his own back by that eye of yours . . .

COLLIE No, no! That weren't him – (*Laughing again*) – be still trying to get his breath back this morning, he will. No, this were Big John, chucker-outerer – well, to *start* with, like . . . it sort of . . . spread after that . . .

JEM You want your heads looking at . . . you'll be ending up in clink one of these days . . .

COLLIE Hey, shame Cheyenne missed it – just his cup of tea . . . stuff flying all over, there was . . . glasses . . . bottles . . . looked like Pilkingtons in a hurricane . . . (*Laughs*)

Ben runs up, panting.

BEN (*eagerly*) I'm here, Mr Clegg! I've fetched it!

JEM Good lad, give it here.

There is a splash as he throws the water.

COLLIE So! Now then! Who've we got here? New recruit?

JEM (*satisfied with the result the water produced*) Aye, that's got it . . . Oh, aye . . . Ben, this here's Collie.

COLLIE Ben is it? (*good naturedly*) Mmm. Need more than half a dozen of *you* to make a pound, wouldn't we, lad?

BEN I suppose so, Mr Collie.

COLLIE (*laughing*) Mister!? You don't have to call *me* mister, young-un – sir'll do. Here! Come on! Let's give the boss a bit of an hand . . . 'fore he gives us both our cards . . .

JEM (*muttering, but he's softened now*) Aye, and not before time some would say . . .

Sounds of shovelling and Collie is singing loudly "Love, Here Is My Song".

COLLIE . . . a serena-ade to yooo." That's it, young-un, hold that open . . . (*More shovelling*)

JEM Here, Collie! Don't have the lad holding them bags like that! He'll have no knuckles left!

COLLIE He's right enough – aren't you, young-un? (*He chuckles*) Get top layer off . . . get down to t'man's skin . . . got hands like a babby . . .

JEM Come here, lad. See! Hold them like this. Right? Then the sacks not rubbing against . . .

BEN Yeah, right, Mr Clegg. Thanks, Mr Clegg . . .

COLLIE See the missus last night, Jem? How's she getting on?

JEM Seems to be mending.

COLLIE Bit better then, is she?

JEM Oh, aye. (*Seeming to realise this was an over-statement*) Well . . . a bit . . . you know.

COLLIE: Right, young-un! Stack them up at the back of the wagon.

Pause and scraping as bag is dragged over the wagon floor. No, you daft . . . ! Not there! You can see the boards is gone there! Daft little . . . !

BEN Sorry, Collie.

COLLIE That's it . . . t'other side! (*To Jem*) 'Bout time them boards had a looking at, Jem . . .

JEM (*Sounding harassed*) Aye. Aye, I'll see it's seen to . . . I'll maybe get round to it . . . Sunday.

COLLIE We'll be losing a bag through that hole if it gets any bigger . . . (*Laughing*) What you might call a "see-through" lorry is ours . . .

JEM (*bad tempered*) Aye, I *said* I'll have a go at it – Sunday . . . after I've visited . . .

COLLIE (*casually*) I'm doing nowt on Sunday – I'll nip over – give you a bit of a hand . . .

JEM Suit yourself, I can do 'em on my own . . .

COLLIE Aye, well, just the same, I'll nip over. (*He laughs to cover his kind thought*) It'll give me a bit of a break from the owd natter-bag. (*Pause*) So, what they say about her then, Jem? The missus?

JEM Nowt much. You know how they are. Don't tell you much. (*He draws the next word out*) Satisfactory – what that's supposed to mean – as if being ill's ever satisfactory . . .

COLLIE Still in the St Christopher is she then?

JEM Aye.

BEN Shall I . . . ? Is it all right to put this here, Mr Clegg?

JEM Shove 'em up a bit, lad – there's another three bags to go there . . .

COLLIE (*as if he could be treading on thin ice*) I was . . . er . . . talking to a fella, you know, he was saying it's supposed to be a bit of all right in the General.

JEM (*not impressed*) Oh, aye.

COLLIE Yea . . . and they looked after our Freda's lad all right in there.

JEM No doubt.

COLLIE I mean . . . you know . . . all I'm saying is . . . it's a dear do is the St Christopher – private like – isn't it?

JEM (*definitely*) She's right enough where she is.

COLLIE (*careful*) Oh, aye. Aye. I was just saying like... they'd look after her all right... at the General... 'stead of you having to fork out...

JEM (*he doesn't raise his voice but puts a very definite end to the conversation*) She's stopping where she is.

COLLIE Aye.

The sound of coal tipping onto the wagon.

Oh, you great daft little...!

BEN I'm sorry! I'm sorry, Mr Clegg! It just sort of...

JEM Well, it'll not jump back into t'sack itself, lad. Here. Cop this shovel!

A voice calls from a short distance.

MAN Hey! Get a move on! *We've* to load up an' all, you know! Come on, Jem! Or are you thinking of stopping for a picnic lunch? That the fastest you can move, Collie?

COLLIE (*shouting back good-naturedly*) Ah, shut your face, Checkers! We'll have this lot going up folks' chimneys and be back for another lot before you've loaded half a dozen bags!

MAN Not at t'rate you lot are going! Come on!

COLLIE (*laughing*) You just see if we don't! We've got young Hercules here! Haven't we, young-un? The demon coal-bagger! He's going to do t'Primrose Estates on his own – aren't you, lad?

BEN (*seriously*) I don't know, Collie.

MAN (*laughing*) Oh, aye! Taking a box to fetch him back in, are you?

COLLIE Naw, he'll do it with one hand! Won't you, nipper?

JEM Right! She's loaded. Finished putting that sack to rights, lad?

BEN Yes, Mr Clegg.

JEM Right. In you jump then.

The cab door is opened.

Are you with us, Collie?

COLLIE (*getting in*) Aye. All aboard for the Sky-Lark! Shove up, young-un!

The cab door is shut and the engine starts. The wagon starts to move off.

Here! Mind your feet, young-un! They're me dancing shoes are these.

BEN Sorry, Collie.

COLLIE (*struggling to get comfortable*) It'll happen be as well if you *don't* get any bigger... we'll never get three of us in this cab.

JEM Pass me that delivery book over, lad.

BEN Er... (*short search*)... this one, Mr Clegg?

JEM Aye, that's it. Hey, look at your knuckles – what did I tell you about...

COLLIE Hey, young-un, don't you go bleeding all over our nice clean cab, *will* you?

BEN No, Collie.

JEM You all right, lad?

BEN Yes, Mr Clegg. I've only grazed...

JEM Aye, you'll be all right. We'll make a coal-bagger out of you yet.

BEN (*excited*) Are we going to tip some coal now, Mr Clegg?

COLLIE No, we're going to ride round all bloody day with it on t'back... silly little...

JEM (*after a short pause*) Oh, take no notice of Collie, lad – he's only having you on, aren't you, Collie?

COLLIE Aye. Here – come on – give-us-a-kiss! (*He grabs Ben.*)

BEN (*embarrassed and angry*) Ger-off!

Jem and Collie laugh and it is only a little while before Ben is laughing with them.

4 A busy housing estate

Sound of heavy boots as Collie approaches Jem who is waiting in the wagon

COLLIE That it, Jem? Four "Best" for Twenty-eight?

JEM Aye, that's it. She pay you?

COLLIE (*chuckling*) Not with anything you could put in t'Post Office.

JME She's *three* week behind now.

COLLIE (*laughing again*) I've been *done* then.

JEM (*never able to resist Collie's easy comicality*) Ttt. If I believed a quarter of the tales *you* tell, you'd be worn to a frazzle by now.

COLLIE Did you not see me limping when I came back just then?

JEM Aye. (*Pause*) Where's the lad got to?

COLLIE (*greatly amused at the thought*) Twenty-four.

JEM Old Hawkeye!? Oh, *no*, we'll be here all bloody day.

COLLIE (*chuckling again*) Every bag you tip you have to stand there while he sifts through it lump by lump for... what is it he call 'em?... "Foreign objects"?

JEM Aye, he thinks we spend two hours at t'coal-yard every mornin' "watering" the nutty-slack down with stones...

COLLIE He marks every bag off on a bit of paper. (*He laughs*) He handed me a brush one day, you know, to sweep up bits as had dropped on to t'path...

JEM Aye?

COLLIE Aye. I told him if he shoved th'andle up me backside, I could sweep up as I came down wi' the bags ...do two jobs at once...

They both laugh as Ben returns.

BEN (*panting heavily*) I put six in at number Twenty-four, Mr Clegg.

JEM Good lad. Hop in. Pay you, did he?

BEN No, Mr Clegg... (*He gulps to get his breath back*)... said he'd see you right Saturday... when you're collecting.

JEM (*sighing*) Aye.

The engine is started up.

What's next, Collie?

Pages being turned.

COLLIE Er... Rosethorn Avenue.

JEM (*hopefully*) Forty-two?

COLLIE Yep.

JEM Thank God for that. I'm gagging for a cup of tea!

They drive off.

5 Kitchen at number 42

A small dog is yapping excitedly.

GRANDMA (*sounding very old*) Is that somebody there?

Outside door is opened.

JEM (*coming in*) Coal, Grandma! You're all right.

COLLIE (*coming in*) Mornin', Grandma! (*The dog yaps again*) Hello! And what's to do with you then, Tinker?

GRANDMA That's enough now, Tinker. It's only Mr Clegg and Colin . . . (*Obviously delighted by their visit*) Come and sit you down both of you. Bit later than usual aren't you, Jemmy? (*fussing happily*) Come on then, sit you down . . . sit you down . . .

JEM Have you a bit of newspaper, Gran? To sit on – then we'll not mess up . . .

GRANDMA You know very well, Jemmy Clegg, I've never minded a bit of muck . . . They haven't invented the dirt yet as can't be fetched off with a drop of water . . .

JEM Aye, but there's no use in messing t'place up, Grandma, not when you keep it as nice as . . .

COLLIE And how's my lovely little raver this week? Missed me have you?

GRANDMA (*teasing back*) Mmm, like a crop of boils. Here you are then . . . here's some paper . . . but I don't mind a bit of muck, you know that very . . .

Rustling of newspaper. Timid knock at the door.

JEM (*calling without hesitation*) Come on in, young-un!

The door is opened and the dog yaps briefly again.

BEN (*timidly*) Mr Clegg?

COLLIE Come on! Come and park yourself!

BEN Oh. Right. Er . . . shall I sit . . . ?

GRANDMA And who've we got here then? You helping Mr Clegg, young man, are you?

BEN I . . . er . . . I just like . . . started . . . today.

GRANDMA You'll be ready for a cup of tea then I dare say . . . (*She struggles to rise from the chair*) I'll put the kettle . . .

JEM Aye, stop where you are, Grandma, I'll see to it.

GRANDMA No you won't, Jemmy Clegg. I've managed to make you a cup of tea for twenty-four years, I'll manage it today. (*She gets up with some considerable effort*) I'm not done-for yet – not by a long chalk . . .

Sound of a kettle being filled.

COLLIE How's them bonny legs of yours this week, Grandma? Fit to come to t'Tropicano for a bit of disco dancing with me, are they?

GRANDMA Oh, they're right enough ... they'll last me till I don't need 'em any more. (*Pause, and then with some concern*) How's your wife, Jemmy? I heard she was ...

JEM Oh, she's mending, Grandma. Well, a *bit*, you know.

GRANDMA They can do a lot these days though, Jemmy, can't they? It's not like ...

JEM (*quickly*) None of that cake of yours going, Grandma? I could eat a bit if ...

GRANDMA (*pleased*) Plenty, Jemmy. Here y'are, open the tin for me ... help yourselves ...

JEM Ta.

GRANDMA No, it's a shame – it is. And you'd never have got started if it hadn't been for her, would you?

JEM No, I wouldn't, Grandma, (*Sighs*) I wouldn't.

GRANDMA Oh, *I* know. Sold everything, didn't she? Everything in t'house? Every stick of furniture? All as she had? So you could buy Tom Baxter's round off him?

JEM She did, Grandma.

COLLIE (*coming to the rescue*) Food for the Gods this currant cake, Grandma. Food for the Gods! Keep on asking you to marry me, don't I, Grandma? But she always turns me down, don't you!?

GRANDMA (*chuckling*) You're as daft as a brush, Colin Anderson. And what in this world happened to your eye?!

COLLIE Wife hit me, Grandma. Proper tartar she is. Knocks me about something shocking ...

GRANDMA Fine tale. I've heard what you get up to, you and that other daft lot down at the Club ... Oh, have a bit bigger piece than that, young ... *what* is it they call you?

BEN Thank you. Er ... Ben.

GRANDMA Ben. Well, you find a nice big piece and I'll wrap you a bit up for later on.

BEN Oh, thanks.

GRANDMA Well, you'll get hungry doing that heavy job. See. There. Put that in your pocket.

BEN Oh, well, it's all right... honest... I...

COLLIE Get it in your pocket.

BEN Th... thank you.

GRANDMA (*to business*) Now then, Jemmy. Put two bags in for me, have you?

JEM I have, Grandma. Two "Best" as always.

GRANDMA Right, here you are then. (*Clink of coins*) I've got it all ready for you. Two bags... Is that the right money?

JEM (*taking the money*) Spot on, Grandma. Ta. You're one of me best payer-upperers.

BEN But, Mr Clegg, I thought two bags...

COLLIE (*quickly*) Want a bit of firewood chopping, Grandma?

GRANDMA Oh, you're all right, Colin, I'm sure you've enough...

COLLIE I'll just do you a few sticks – on the way out – not take a minute...

GRANDMA Well, if you would, Colin, but I'm sure you've plenty to do without...

COLLIE Mind you, Grandma, the price is a kiss or another piece of that there currant-cake...

GRANDMA You'll have to settle for the cake, Colin Anderson, as well *you* know...

COLLIE (*sighing dramatically*) Ah, well... cake it'll have to be then... (*He munches*) Mmm. Grandma Beeton they should call you...

GRANDMA (*laughing*) Go on, be off with you. You'll eat me out of house and home, all you great big fellas...

Scraping of chair.

JEM Right. Best be off, Grandma. Thanks for the tea.

GRANDMA You're welcome, Jemmy.

JEM Come on, you two! Let's get this last few dropped and get back to the yard for dinner before we load up again...

The other two get up and they all move to the door.

COLLIE See you in a fortnight then, Beautiful! (*He blows a kiss*) And don't be having any other men in while I'm gone.

GRANDMA (*enjoying the joke*) Get off with you.

BEN Er... thank you... for the cake.

GRANDMA You be a good boy for Mr Clegg now – help him proper.

JEM Take care of yourself, Grandma.

The men go out and close the door. The dog yaps again.

GRANDMA (*sighing and settling down again*) Come on, Tinker. That's enough. You don't have to bark – at visitors.

6 The wagon

Collie climbs into the cab where Jem and Ben are sitting waiting.

JEM Do her wood for her, Collie?

COLLIE Yeah, she'll have enough to last her.

JEM Right. (*The engine starts up.*) Just make these last few drops and then...

BEN (*uncertainly*) Mr Clegg?

JEM Aye?

BEN I... I think I must have charged that man too much in Maple Crescent...

JEM You're all right, lad. You took the right money.

BEN But... but, Mr Clegg. That old lady only gave you ...

COLLIE Here! Blockhead! You got any other reason for having your gob open? Other than talking, I mean?

BEN (*surprised and bewildered*) No, Collie.

COLLIE Right then. Shut it!

BEN Oh. (*Pause*) Right, Collie.

The wagon pulls away.

7 The yard

The men jump out of the wagon and the cab doors bang shut.

JEM Right, lad. Just stack them bags up a bit better and when you've done that you can come in and have some dinner. Lightnin' will have some tea on – if you can call it that...

BEN Right, Mr Clegg.

COLLIE Peas, lad?

BEN You what, Collie?

COLLIE (*incredulous*) "You what"? To *me*? And me dad's a Bobby? I *said*, Little Sir Blockhead, do you want *peas*? With your fish and chips?

BEN Fish and chips?

COLLIE (*groaning*) Oh, hell! What've you got between your ears? Where your brains is supposed to be?! Fish and chips! (*Explaining as to an idiot child*) I'm going to the chippy. For us dinners. And you can have fish and chips and peas *or* fish and chips and *no* peas. Now! Do you *want* bloody peas!?

BEN No, thanks, Collie.

COLLIE (*sighing*) Right. And *you* can go and get 'em tomorrow – now you've taken over the post of Junior Executive.

JEM (*calling back*) Ask 'em to do a fish without batter for me, Collie! Me stomach's playing up.

COLLIE (*shouting back*) It's high time you saw somebody about that.

JEM I will! This afternoon! I'll get a bottle of "herbal" off old Jack-cum-Tomorrow!

Jem goes into the "office" and shuts door.

BEN Who's Jack-cum-Tomorrow?

COLLIE Chemist. Blackerman Street. Name's Jack. (*Jingling money*) One fish, chips and peas, one...

BEN But why do they call him...?

COLLIE Aren't you supposed to be stacking them bags?

BEN Yeah, but...

COLLIE (*as he moves away*) No peas then.

BEN But...?

COLLIE (*calling back*) ... because he never has anything you ask for, blockhead! When you go in!

BEN (*huh?*) Oh. (*Eventually he gets it*) Oh!

8 The "office"

CHEYENNE (*talking with his mouth full*) . . . Anyway, I can't see 'em beating Halifax, not with . . . (*The door opens*). Hello! If it's not Little Weed! You made it till dinner-time then? How's your back then, Little Weed?

BEN 'S'all right.

CHEYENNE (*laughing*) You'll not think so – in t'mornin'.

JEM The lad's not done so bad, Cheyenne. He's earnt his dinner any road. Pour the lad a sup of tea, Lightnin'.

LIGHTNIN' Aaay. It's not the bloody . . .

JEM Aye. Aye. We know . . .

The door opens again.

COLLIE (*coming in*) Luncheon is served, gentlemen. Now, who's is the one without petit pois? Ah, yes, the young sir, I do believe. Here! Cop hold o' that!

JEM Come on, Collie, I'm clem't. Did you get me fish with no batter?

COLLIE Most certainly, sir. Hiya, Cheyenne. You missed a good "do" last night.

CHEYENNE I didn't! There was a beltin' John Wayne on. Cast of thousands . . . in *colour*. (*He laughs*) You look like you could have been in it. What happened to your eye? Get too close to t'go-go dancer? (*They all laugh*)

COLLIE Got too close to Big John's bunch of fives.

CHEYENNE (*impressed*) Big John? You're lucky your back's not in a splint. (*Pause*) Oh, aye, Jem. Raptash were looking for you.

JEM Oh, aye.

CHEYENNE Aye. Said he'd catch you when he got back from his dinner.

JEM (*sighing*) Aye. I bet he will. (*He laughs*) Hey! Young-un! You going fifteen rounds with that cod or what?

BEN (*gulping down the food as fast as he can*) You what, Mr Clegg?

CHEYENNE Looks like you've given the lad an appetite, Jem.

JEM He's not done so bad. You straighten them bags up, like I told you?

BEN Yes, Mr Clegg.

JEM Good lad.

BEN Oh, and there was some planks of wood, Mr Clegg ... under the bags ... I straightened them up and all. Funny, I didn't see them this morning when we set off...

COLLIE (*laughing*) No, you wouldn't. They fell onto t'back of the lorry – when we was passing Entwistle's woodyard.

BEN (*innocently*) Did they, Collie? (*They all laugh*).

CHEYENNE Bit of luck that, Jem. (*Laughs*) And your bottom boards needing replacing.

JEM Aye. (*Laughing*) What you might call a lucky co-in-cydence.

They all laugh again. The door opens.

COLLIE 'Lo there, Joe!

JOE CLOG (*coming in*) Hiya, Collie. 'Lo, Jem. Saw Raptash when I was walking home, said ...

JEM Aye, I know.

COLLIE (*smirking*) What she give you for your dinner then, Joe?

JOE CLOG Well, it didn't get served up with chips and peas, I'll tell you that.

CHEYENNE (*laughing*) It's to be hoped you took your clogs off first. (*To the others*) Only been married four month and he's three stone lighter now. If she doesn't get fed up soon he'll be droppin' down a grid.

They all laugh. Door opens again.

RAPTASH (*coming in*) Good day, gentlemen.

CHEYENNE Oh, hello, Rap... Mr Merrick. Have a nice dinner, did you?

RAPTASH A very pleasant lunch, thank you. I hope you're all enjoying yours, gentlemen...? Ah, Mr Clegg, you're there. I wonder if I might just have a word or two? If you've finished your...

JEM Well, I *would* like, but... well, er... I was thinking to make an early start, Mr Merrick... seeing we were a bit late this mornin' and...

RAPTASH Well, if you could just step into the back... I won't keep you more than...

JEM (*sighing resignation and getting up*) Aye. Right-o.

RAPTASH (*as they go into the other room*) I won't hold you up...

just a quick word... (*As he closes the door*) You see, strictly speaking...

The door closes behind them.

COLLIE Jumped-up, bloody-little...

JOE CLOG What's he want with Jem, anyway?

COLLIE Well, there's one thing for certain, Joe Clog, he's not in there telling him the Asherton Coal Company's giving free coal to its oldest customers this week.

CHEYENNE Aye. (*He sighs*) You've heard it's going up again?

COLLIE (*groaning*) Oh no! I hates it when they put it up. You ask 'em for the money and folk look at you like you've put it up yourself so you can have your villa in t'South of France redecorated...

CHEYENNE Aye – and then they don't pay you. Do you know, I've *one* – she owes me *sixteen* weeks now. "I'll pay you as soon as the baby's born," she says, "with the maternity grant..."

COLLIE Don't leave her any more!

CHEYENNE I said that! Couple of weeks back... started cryin' on t'doorstep – had all the street out she did – all calling me not fit to live they were – leaving a pregnant women wi'out coal...

COLLIE (*chuckling*) Got you by the short and curlies, hasn't she? You'd just better hope her babby's not late...

CHEYENNE (*laughing*) Aye. I can just see it now – two of us pacing up and down outside the labour ward – its father... and *me*... with me collecting book!

COLLIE (*laughing*) Aye. (*Screwing up his chip paper*) Here! Young-un! Want some chips? Too fatty for me. Reckon the old chip boiler's ready for a 50,000 mile oil change...

BEN Oh. Yeah! Thanks, Collie!

COLLIE Get 'em down you then... Build you up.

CHEYENNE Hey! I'll tell you what, Little Weed... *I'll* show you summat as'll build you up. Come on outside and I'll show you...

JOE CLOG Hammer trick, you mean, Cheyenne?

CHEYENNE Come on, Little Weed!

BEN I haven't finished me chips, Cheyenne.

CHEYENNE Never mind your chips – this'll put more meat on

you. (*He opens door*) Come on! Come on, Joe. Coming, Collie?

COLLIE Oh yea, coming, Cheyenne. (*Getting up*) Just wondering what old Raptash is up to in there with Jem. He's been a long time...

CHEYENNE Happen showing him his etchings. (*As they go out, confidentially*) He's...er...he's...all right, i'n't he? Jem? Not...well...not in any bother wi' brass or owt?

COLLIE (*unsure*) No. No, I don't think... (*Dismissing any doubts*) Naw, he's never been more than a week late with his coal money – not Jem – not since *I've* worked for him anyroad.

CHEYENNE Well, you know, I just thought...you know, he's ...all right is Jem. And what with his missus and ...if he's short of a bob or two...

JOE CLOG (*cautioning*) You thinking of asking him if he wants a hand-out, are you, Cheyenne? 'Cause you might find it hard work walking around with no head on your shoulders...

CHEYENNE I was only *saying*...

COLLIE Joe's right, Cheyenne – for *once* – I'd think twice if I were you. You know he's not the sort as would thank you for...

CHEYENNE All right! All right! (*Pause*) But...do you think he'd *say* though? If he needed a bit of help like? He got me started you know, I wouldn't like to see... Do you think he'd *say*?

COLLIE Oh, aye! Certainly! Nothing more definite! (*Pause*) Hey! Cheyenne! See that!?

CHEYENNE What? What?

COLLIE Great big pig it were! Flew right over the top of your lorry!

CHEYENNE Ttt. Clever clogs. (*Pause as the others laugh*) And what *you* staring at, Little Weed!?

BEN I wasn't, Cheyenne! I was just waiting for...

CHEYENNE What for!?

BEN You...you said you were going to show me something. To build me up.

CHEYENNE Oh. Aye. So I am, Little Weed. So I am. Here y'are, Joe! Pass us that fifty-six pound hammer!

9 The yard

A few minutes later. Sound of Cheyenne straining, relaxing and then there is a heavy thud.

CHEYENNE Right! Got it, Little Weed? That's all there is to it!

BEN (*sounding worried*) I don't think I . . . I think it's a bit too heavy . . .

JOE CLOG Aye, you can do it, Little Weed! Cheyenne's taught hundreds to do this! Haven't you, Cheyenne?

CHEYENNE Aye. Nothing to it! Come on. Here. See. You just put the hammer head-down at the side of you – at arms' length . . . see? Right. Now. You put one arm out straight to the side and take hold of the top of the handle . . . right? Now, you have to keep your arm straight – just use your wrist – like this, see? And then you lift – bring the head up and over . . . and then towards you . . . (*He takes a deep breath*) . . . and . . . down . . . slowly . . . 'til the hammer-head touches your lips . . . See? And then back over again . . . (*Thud*) See? Nowt to it!

BEN But you've got bigger arms than me, Cheyenne!

CHEYENNE Well how do you think I got 'em!? Doing the hammer-trick. Didn't I, Joe?

JOE CLOG Aye. 'S right, Little Weed. Come on. You can do it. Grab hold . . . keep your arm stretched out . . . Now . . . that's it . . . grasp the handle . . . good grip . . . Now! You've nearly got the head upright now . . .

Ben is puffing with the exertion. Suddenly Jem is heard shouting from a short distance.

JEM Hey! What the . . . !? Drop it! Drop it, you silly little . . . ! (*Thud*)

CHEYENNE (*as Jem joins the group*) Just showing him the hammer-trick, Jem.

BEN (*puffing and excited*) I think I could have done it, Mr Clegg. Can I have another go?

JEM I'm bloody surprised at you, Collie. Standing there letting 'em . . .

BEN I think I could have done it, Mr Clegg.

JEM I should have thought – *you* of all folk, Collie . . . Fancy standing there watching 'em . . .

CHEYENNE Only a bit of fun, Jem... We meant the lad no harm.

BEN It wasn't Collie's fault, Mr Clegg! It were *me*, I said I'd have a go... Collie never...

JOE CLOG Lad's telling the truth, Jem. It were me and Cheyenne. Collie never...

JEM Show him, Collie! Go on! Show the lad!

COLLIE Nay, Jem... we didn't mean the lad any... it were only a bit of fun...

JEM (*still angry*) Bit of fun? Aye, you show him! Go on! Take 'em out, Collie! Show him!

Pause.

BEN (*astonished*) False teeth! Are they *all* false, Collie?

JEM Aye, they are! (*Impatiently*) Oh, put 'em back in! You look like Ena Sharples. And *that's* what *you'd* 'a' looked like... if I hadn't stopped you!

BEN But... but, Mr Clegg...

JEM It was *his* first day and some clever bugger showed *him* the hammer-trick. See, lad, once you get fifty-six pounds of weight up above you in the air like that you really have to know what you're doing – otherwise it comes down towards you a bloody lot faster than you can stop it.

BEN Oh.

JEM Aye. "Oh". And nobody bothered telling Collie that and it came down and knocked every one of his teeth out.

BEN Oh. (*Short pause*) Did it hurt, Collie?

COLLIE (*making a sound that registers disbelief*) Oh... (*Frustrated*) Oh, come on! Let's get some bloody work done!

10 The wagon

Sounds of loading.

COLLIE (*puffing slightly*) Right, young-un! Shove that to the back... Are we taking a full load, Jem?

JEM (*calling back*) 'Course we are! Unless you're thinking of going on short time...!

COLLIE Aye. Righty-o! Here y'are, young-un.

BEN Right, Collie. (*He heaves a bag.*) Where will we be delivering this afternoon, Mr Clegg?

JEM Oh, we're doing the posh end this afternoon, lad. Best houses – worst payers. Groveland Avenue... all round that sort of...

COLLIE Better round there in t'summer, mind you... when all them wives is out sunning themselves in their gardens... (*He chuckles*)

A mournful voice is coming closer.

LIGHTNIN' Clegg! Aaay, deary me. (*He groans with the effort of walking*) Jemmy Clegg! Anybody seen...?

COLLIE It's Lightnin', Jem. Looking for you. (*He calls*) Over here, Lightnin'!

LIGHTNIN' (*joining them now*) Jem Clegg. Telephone. For you.

JEM For me?

LIGHTNIN' (*exhausted*) Aaay. Aye. Telephone. For thee. Aaay. I don't know what that yon Merrick thinks I am. Running all over. Taking messages (*He wanders off again*) ... fetching and carrying... Aaay...

JEM Finish loading up, Collie. I'd best go and see what...

He walks away.

COLLIE Right-oh, Jem. (*He calls*) Who do you reckon's ringing you up...?

JEM (*at a fair distance now*) Well, there's only one road of finding out...

COLLIE (*teasing*) Be one of them there girlfriends of yours ... (*Jem is out of earshot*) Right. Come on, then, young-un – you heard what the boss said – shift yourself! (*He sings loudly and cheerfully*) "You get a little drunk and you land in jail..."

11 The cab of the wagon

Collie and Ben are sitting waiting.

COLLIE Wonder where Jem's got to? He's been ages. (*Pause*) Want a smoke, young-un?

BEN No. I don't, Collie.

COLLIE Oi. No, I don't, Collie – *what*?

BEN (*in all innocence*) No, I don't smoke, Collie.

COLLIE (*blowing out and then whistling in a bored kind of way*) Drink, do you?

BEN No, Collie.

COLLIE Follow the gee-gees?

BEN No, Collie.

COLLIE (*hopefully*) Take lassies out? Behind the pavilion?

BEN No. (*short pause*) Well... only one or two like...

COLLIF Thank God for that! I was thinking of writing to t' Pope about you...

Heavy footsteps approaching.

Ah, 'bout time too. Shove up. Make some room for our chauffeur. (*He whistles*) By heck, by the look on his face he must have had the Tax Man after him ...

Cab door is opened.

All right, Jem?

JEM (*curtly*) Are we loaded?

BEN Yes, Mr Clegg, Collie and me...

JEM (*very abruptly*) Right!

He gets in and slams the door loudly. Engine starts and wagon moves off.

COLLIE We doing Groveland Avenue then, Jem?

JEM (*angrily*) I *said*, didn't I?! You want it in bloody writing or what?!

COLLIE All right, all right. Bloody hell!

The wagon accelerates away noisily.

Fade out

12 The estate

Sound of two pairs of heavy boots on gravel and then coal being tipped.

COLLIE Six! Phew, I don't know how it is – every bag gets heavier after four o'clock.

Jem walks away.

JEM (*sharply*) Come on! Another six yet! We're leaving everybody double this week!

COLLIE (*puzzled*) Double!? What...? (*Calling louder as Jem is a fair distance away by now*) Here! What for!?

JEM (*calling back*) Because I bloody *said* so!

COLLIE (*muttering as he plods after Jem*) What the hell's got ...? And to think, I very nearly decided on being a brain surgeon...

13 Further along the estate

Cab door opening. Ben is climbing in to join Jem and Collie.

BEN (*tired but still enthusiastic*) I've done that, Mr Clegg. Four bags for number...

JEM (*sounds more weary than angry now*) Right. Shut the door then, lad.

Door banged shut.

Right. Next avenue...

Wagon drives off.

COLLIE Here you are, lad. Have a sup of this...

BEN Oh. No, thanks, Collie.

COLLIE Here y'are, *have* some! It's only tea. I got that bird at number seventeen to fill me flask up for me – couldn't get owt else off her. Here! Take a drink...

BEN (*sounds rather odd*) No, 's all right, Collie. Honest.

COLLIE What's up with you? You must be thirsty. You'll have a sup, Jem?

JEM Ta, Collie. (*He drinks*) Ta. Here y'are.

COLLIE Ta. Come on, young-un, she makes a good brew does number seventeen – plenty sugar in it...

BEN No, I... (*He coughs*) I... I don't think I want any ...

JEM You all right, young-un?

BEN Yeah. (*Pause*) I just... (*Another pause*) Is there...? Is there any... toilets round here, Mr Clegg?

COLLIE (*laughing*) I thought you were a bit red in t' face. (*He laughs again*) Have you been sitting there dying for a pee and not saying...? Why di'n't you just...?

BEN (*embarrassed*) Well, I... I kept keeping a look out ... as we went round...

COLLIE What for!?

BEN Well... you know... a toilet...

COLLIE (*laughing*) You sure you wouldn't like one with a shower as well...?

The engine slows and idles.

JEM Oh, leave the lad alone, Collie, you're nought but a big daft kid at times...

COLLIE Well! Go on!

BEN (*confused*) Go on what?

COLLIE Go on! What you waiting for!

BEN But...?

COLLIE Get behind that wall there. What's up!? Waiting for me to come and hold your hand...?

BEN (*jumping down*) Oh. Yeah. Right. (*He runs off*) I'll not be a minute, Mr Clegg...

COLLIE (*chuckling as he watches Ben run off*) Daft little beggar ... Fancy him sitting wi' his legs together... (*He chuckles*) Don't seem like a bad lad though.

JEM (*who has not been listening*) Huh?

COLLIE Young-un. I said, we've had *worse*. (*No response*) Helpers!... We've had...

JEM (*as if out of a trance suddenly*) Oh, aye. Aye.

COLLIE Seems honest at any rate. (*He laughs*) Here, remember the one we had as pocketed old Mrs Nelligan's coal money?

JEM (*still obviously not concentrating*) Aye. (*Giving a poor imitation of being amused*) Aye, I do.

COLLIE He must have known she'd tell us she'd paid the following week. Daft little so-and-so.. (*Laughing*) I thought she were going to murder him with that yard brush... remember, Jem? Chasing him up the Entry...

The cab door opens.

BEN (*getting in*) I'm here, Mr Clegg.

COLLIE Aye, we can see...

The wagon starts to move off again.

...and about three pints lighter by the look of you. Righty-o, then. Where we off to now? Let's have a look... (*Turning the pages of the delivery book*) Woodcock Avenue...twenty-eight, thirty, thirty-four... thirty-six is on holiday.

BEN (*shouting*) Mr Clegg! Look out!

The brakes squeal and there is a yelp from outside on the road.

COLLIE What the...?!

BEN (*shouting*) You hit it, Mr Clegg! You hit it!

COLLIE What!? What was it...!?

JEM (*wearily*) A dog. It just ran into t'...

The cab door opens.

BEN (*getting out*) You hit it, Mr. Clegg! You hit it real hard!

He runs around to the front of the wagon.

COLLIE (*without much concern – he calls*) Just shove it to t' side, young-un...

BEN It's only a puppy, Mr Clegg!

COLLIE (*bored by the delay*) Shove it onto t'pavement, lad.

BEN (*shouting again*) It's not dead, Mr Clegg! It's not dead! Collie! Come and have a look! I think it'll be all right! Come and...

The dog sets up a pitiful whine.

JEM (*calling*) Get out the way!

BEN See! See! It's not dead, Mr Clegg! Just come and ...

JEM (*forcefully now*) Come out the way, lad!

The engine revs up.

BEN What you doing, Mr Clegg!? Where're you...?! Mr Clegg! What are you...!?

COLLIE Shift, young-un! We're backing up! Mind yourself ...!

BEN But what...?!

COLLIE Will you *move*!? The thing's *had* it! We'll finish it off!

BEN (*almost screaming*) No!

COLLIE It'll be better off! Listen to it! Let Jem finish it...

BEN (*near to weeping now*) No! Don't! Please, Mr Clegg! Don't!

JEM It's the best thing, lad... You can't let it...

Ben comes rushing around to Jem's cab window.

BEN (*sounding very young and frightened*) Please, Mr Clegg! Don't, Mr Clegg! Don't run it over again! It'll be all right.

The dog's cries can still be heard.

JEM See, lad, just listen to the poor little beggar... It'll not feel owt – it'll be better off if I just...

The engine revs again, threateningly.

BEN (*hysterical*) No! I won't let you! I won't!

COLLIE (*he's had enough of this*) Oh, stop being a babby! It's only a bloody dog! There's thousands of strays round here...

BEN (*pleading now*) *I'll* look after it, Mr Clegg. Let me ...! Let me take it home... I'm good with animals. I'll see to it.

JEM Nay, lad. It'll only die and if it *lives* it'll be no good to nobody – not after being hit wi' this thing... best to put an end to it...

BEN Please! No! Mr Clegg, I can look after it... honest! I *can*... just let me...

COLLIE Ay, this is daft this is...

BEN (*desperate*) I mended our cat's leg – I did, Mr Clegg! I'm good wi' animals... Don't kill it, Mr Clegg... Don't...

There is a silence for a moment.

JEM (*sighing*) Oh... go on then. Lift it on t'back... Put a sack or summat over it...

BEN (*relieved beyond proper expression*) Yeah! Yeah! I will, I will, Mr Clegg. I'll put it on the back, Mr Clegg. It'll be all right when I get it home. You'll see, I'll look after it...

COLLIE (*disgruntled*) Ttt. Be all right if we go round picking up everything we run over – be like bloody Noah's Ark it will.

JEM (*calling to Ben in a tired voice*) Come on, lad. Get a move on... we've work to do and all, you know.

BEN I'm coming, Mr Clegg! (*Tenderly to the dog*) Nay, nay, it's all right. Sssh. Sssh. See, we'll just put you up here... There... See. (*The dog is still crying*) Hush. Hush. See, I'll cover you up. (*The dog settles somewhat*) Aye. That's it. That's it. Ben'll see to you...

COLLIE Come on!

Ben comes back round and climbs into the cab. The door closes.

BEN It'll be all right, Mr Clegg. You'll see, it'll be...

COLLIE (*sullenly*) Bloody thing'll be dead afore you get it home.

BEN It'll not!

COLLIE Bet you.

JEM Oh, leave him alone, Collie. (*He sighs. The wagon moves off*) ... Let him try if he wants ...

COLLIE It's not right, letting it suffer ...

JEM (*angrily*) I said *leave him be*! If it dies it dies ... (*More quietly*) ... but at least he'll have ...

COLLIE (*sulking*) It'll only *die*.

BEN It'll not! It'll not!

JEM (*angry and frustrated*) Oh ... shut up!!

Wagon driving away.

14 The cab

The wagon is moving along steadily. Jem and Collie are speaking more softly than usual. Both men are subdued and Collie is giving a weak imitation of his usual brightness.

COLLIE You don't have to drop me at the yard, Jem – your place'll do. You'll be wanting to ...

JEM (*gently*) Aye, right-o, Collie ... if you're sure. (*Trying to sound bright*) Out tonight, are you?

COLLIE (*he's trying, too*) Yeah, I might just force myself to nip down to t'club for the last hour or so ... if she'll let me out ... (*He attempts a chuckle but it doesn't quite come off*)

JEM Still asleep, is he?

COLLIE (*chuckling softly*) Aye. Well away. Like a babby. I thought his legs was going to buckle with that last bag he hoisted ...

JEM He's not done so bad.

COLLIE (*without any malice*) Well, he weren't much help on them last three streets. Conked out just after Gonnall Close ...

JEM Well, we've had 'em as didn't last *that* long. Ttt. Look at the little beggar's hands ... looks like he's been walking on *them* 'stead of his feet.

COLLIE He'll harden up – after a week or two. He'll be shifting with the best of us before the month's out ...

JEM Aye.

COLLIE (*after a short pause*) I'll see to the collecting for you on Saturday then, Jem, like you said ...

JEM If you would, Collie. If you would.

COLLIE And if... well... if there's owt else you want... you know... till you get yourself sorted out like... (*the sentence dying of embarrassment*) you know...?

JEM Aye. I know.

COLLIE Well... till you... get sorted out...

JEM Aye... er... thanks like... you know...

COLLIE (*glad of an opportunity to put an end to this conversation*) Here we are then! Home! Another day over and done with.

JEM Give the lad a shake, Collie.

The wagon comes to a halt.

COLLIE Come on then, Sleeping Beauty – or are you waiting for a kiss?

BEN Mmm. Mmm?

COLLIE (*amused*) Come on, you can wake up now! We've done it all for thee – we're home.

BEN (*coming to with a jolt now*) What? Eh? Oh. I fell asleep. I'm sorry, Mr Clegg, I must have...

Cab door opens.

JEM You're all right, lad, you didn't do so bad... for a beginner.

BEN I'm sorry, Mr Clegg... I don't remember going to sleep. (*Short pause*) Did you manage all right without me?

COLLIE Well, we found it hard going like, you know, didn't we, Jem? But we managed to struggle through. (*Giving him a shove*) Come on. Out you get, youngun.

They jump down and shut the cab door.

You want to get your Mam to soak them hands for you when you get home...

JEM Aye... and make sure you get 'em cleaned proper... all them grazes... otherwise they'll fester...

BEN (*refreshed after his sleep*) I'll do that, Mr Clegg. I will. They'll be all right for the morning...

JEM Good lad... and don't be late, will you? I want to get off if we're delivering double this week...

BEN No, I'll be here in good time, Mr Clegg. (*Starts to move away*) Oh. The dog. I nearly forgot him... Can I take one of these sacks to put round him, Mr Clegg?

JEM No.

BEN (*surprised*) I'll fetch it back tomorrow – honest. It's just to keep him warm like...just while I get him ...

JEM You don't need no sack for him.

BEN But...but it's important, Mr Clegg... Keeping 'em warm... I'll fetch it back in the mornin' – honest.

COLLIE (*flatly*) Dog's dead, young-un.

BEN (*stunned*) What?

JEM (*seemingly careless*) Go on, you get off home, lad. I'll bury it in t'...

BEN (*upset*) But what happened to it?! It were all right last time I...

COLLIE Come on, young-un, get yourself off home. Have a bath. It's been a long enough day – *I'm* beggared even if you're not...

BEN But...?

COLLIE We'll see it gets buried. Go on – go and get your tea...

BEN No. I want to know what... I want to see it!

Ben runs to the rear to the wagon.

COLLIE (*calling*) Come away! What you want to see it for? Bloody thing's dead! (*To himself*) Oh, Hell-fire.

Ben gives a small hurt cry when he reaches the dog. There is silence as he walks slowly back to the two men. When he speaks he is crying.

BEN You've killed it. Haven't you? You've bloody killed it.

COLLIE (*lamely*) I *haven't*. It...it...died. Oh, it never had a chance anyway. It's better off...

JEM (*sounding like he's about to drop with fatigue*) See, come on, lad. Leave it there, Collie and me'll bury it... You go and...

BEN (*all the tiredness flooding back now*) What did you do it for? I could have looked after it. I could. Look at it. It were only a pup. It would have been all right. You wrung its neck, didn't you?

COLLIE I didn't.

BEN (*angry now*) You did! I...I hate you! You did!

JEM He didn't, lad.

BEN He did! I can tell! He did!

JEM He *didn't*. (*Pause*) I did.

(*Silence*)

BEN (*sniffing pathetically*) You, Mr Clegg?

JEM Aye. Now go on home!

(*Starts to walk away*) ... and I'll see thee in the mornin' ...

BEN (*anger overcoming the surprise*) You won't! I'm not coming! I'm *never* coming!

JEM (*has walked away but the complete weariness he feels carries the distance*) Aye, well... suit yourself... suit yourself. (*A couple more steps*) See you in t'mornin', Collie.

COLLIE Aye. See you, Jem. (*Turning on Ben*) And I'll see *thee* an' all!

BEN You'll not! (*He shouts angrily after Jem again now*) You shouldn't have done that, Mr Clegg! You shouldn't have! (*Spluttering with childlike frustration*) And... and I'm *telling*... I'm telling... about you and them planks... You pinched 'em, di'n't you?

COLLIE (*quietly but sounding pretty menacing*) That'll do, young-un. Tha's said enough.

BEN (*almost scared off*) Well... he shouldn't have... and he shouldn't have killed it! What did you *let* him for?

COLLIE Look, lad, there's things you don't know...

BEN But why? Why'd he do it!?

COLLIE See. He couldn't stand it crying, that's all. (*Struggling with impatience, anger and sympathy*) It... it started up cryin' when you'd gone asleep. He... he just couldn't stand listening to it... that's all... He just...

BEN He'd no right! I said I'd look after...

COLLIE Come on. 'S no use in going on about it... I'll walk home with you...

BEN No! (*Starts to run*) No. I don't want you to! (*As he runs faster*) ... I hate you! I hate you all! You're all ... (*As if he's splitting out the ultimate insult*) ... horrible!

COLLIE (*calling*) Here! Hang on! I want to tell you...

BEN (*from a good distance now*) No! (*A few more strides*) You're all horrible! ... And... and I don't *want* to be a coal-bagger...!

COLLIE (*as he walks after Ben*) Ay, what a day. (*Sighs*) It's days like this that gets living a bad name...

15 The yard (next morning)

Jem and Collie are getting into the cab. The doors slam shut and Jem starts the engine.

COLLIE Right! All loaded up, Boss... and I've signed us out.

JEM Right.

COLLIE So, you'll do the works orders with me this morning then and I'll finish off on me own this afternoon?

JEM Manage all right, will you?

COLLIE Manage!? Me!? The bionic coal-man!? (*Not so lightly now*) Aye, I'll be all right, Jem. You get off and do what you have to...

JEM It's just... there's 'arrangements', you know... 'arrangements'...

COLLIE Aye.

The wagon starts to move off slowly.

Didn't turn in then? Young-un?

JEM No. I gave him a few minutes, like.

COLLIE Aye. (*Pause*) Aye, well, we can manage without having to change nappies on t'way round...

JEM Not a bad lad though... shame I had to... it would only have suffered, you know...

COLLIE I tried catching him up like but... Ttt. Daft though – all that fuss over a bloody... Anyroad, there's plenty more lads where he came from...

JEM Aye. (*Back to business*) Right then. We'll do Dye Works first... eighteen they want... and then...

Ben runs up calling for them to stop.

BEN Mr Clegg! Wait! Mr Clegg!

The wagon's engine slows to a stop and Ben reaches them. He's panting wildly from the run.

COLLIE Hey-up, young-un.

BEN (*hardly able to breathe*) Mr Clegg... me Mam told me... Mr Clegg... I didn't know about... you never said...

COLLIE What sort of bloody time do you call this to turn up? It's not the night-shift, you know.

BEN (*still panting*) Mr Clegg... you never said... I didn't...

JEM No matter, lad.

BEN ... with you not saying... (*Tries to regain some composure*) Me Mam and Dad... says to tell you they was very sorry to hear and (*He falters*) ... and... if you want anything just...

JEM (*in place of thanks*) Aye.

BEN ... And they said will you let them know what day it'll be on and...

JEM I'll see they get to know, lad.

BEN (*still a little out of puff*) ... and me Mam says I've to tell you how daft it were... me running off and saying... anyway, she says... I've to... I've got to say... I'm sorry.

JEM Aye, well! You don't want to take too much notice of women, lad. They'll have you saying all sorts of rubbish. Now! You coming, ... or what!?

BEN Oh. Right. Yea!

Short pause

COLLIE Well!?

BEN (*innocently*) Well, what, Collie?

COLLIE Well what you standing there for then? Ger-in!

BEN Oh! Yeah. Right!

Ben jumps up into the cab. The wagon moves off.

JEM How's them hands of yours? Sore, are they?

BEN (*unconvincingly*) No! No, Mr Clegg. (*Short pause*) Well... a bit like...

COLLIE (*chuckling softly*) Not to worry – first ten years is the worst. That right, Jem?

JEM (*chuckling*) Aye.

BEN (*happy to be back*) Me Mam said I should put some gloves on... but I told her... (*In an unintentionally comical 'tough-guy', scathing tone*) ... Coal-baggers don't wear *gloves*!

Collie starts to chuckle delightedly. Jem joins in and then, not quite knowing why, Ben starts to laugh too.

Fade out

Home Truths

Peter Whalley

The Cast

Mirabelle

Mark

Mrs Baldwin

Mr Baldwin

Lynn

Father Drabble

Home Truths

1 A train carriage

Sound of a train, modern, electric, travelling at high speed.

MIRABELLE (*tentatively*) Mark?

MARK Huh?

MIRABELLE Oh, I thought you were asleep.

MARK (*yawning*) No, I can never sleep on trains.

MIRABELLE You looked as though you were asleep.

MARK Just half an hour to go.

MIRABELLE It hasn't seemed long, has it?

MARK That's the trouble with these high-speed trains. All those posters telling people to go and see one another. Means you've no excuse for not going.

MIRABELLE (*gently reproving*) Mark!

MARK A joke. Just a joke.

MIRABELLE Do you want this?
Rustle of newspaper.
I've finished with it.

MARK No thanks. I've gone off newspapers.

MIRABELLE What have they done to you?

MARK They're . . . er . . . transient.

MIRABELLE Really?

MARK Yes. And they cost too much.

MIRABELLE I thought you might allow yourself the odd column during vacation.

MARK No.

MIRABELLE (*with a rustle of paper*) Go back to sleep then.

MARK I wasn't asleep. They read the *Daily Express* you know.

MIRABELLE Pardon?

MARK My parents. The whole house'll be knee-deep in papers. *Daily Express, Evening Star, Universe . . .*

MIRABELLE *Universe?*

MARK It's Catholic.

MIRABELLE It sounded . . . galactic. I didn't know there were Catholic papers. I mean special Catholic papers.

MARK Special Catholic everything.

MIRABELLE What did you tell them about me?

MARK Oh, just that you were a friend of mine. Same college . . . and fancied tasting the delights of Padiham during your Easter holidays.

MIRABELLE Just a friend?

MARK A girlfriend. I said a girlfriend in the letter.

MIRABELLE A girlfriend?

MARK The girlfriend.

MIRABELLE Thank you. (*Pause*) You haven't said anything about the flat?

MARK What? Our flat?

MIRABELLE Yes.

MARK Good God, no!

MIRABELLE What have you told them then?

MARK Oh, that I share with a friend. They presume I mean another male. At least I presume that they presume I mean another male.

MIRABELLE I see. And am I supposed to know him?

MARK Oh, they won't ask any awkward questions, don't worry.

MIRABELLE Suppose they ever decided to come down to see you?

MARK Then you'd have to get your hair cut, put a pair of trousers on and do something about your . . .

MIRABELLE We'd better hope they don't then, hadn't we?

MARK They won't.

MIRABELLE So my official role is The Girlfriend.

MARK Yes. When I said you were coming, mother wrote back and said (*Imitating his mother*), "Dear Mark, it's grand to know that you're courting and it'll be lovely to meet Mirabelle. I trust, of course, that she is a good Catholic girl and not one of these modern types. Love, mum."

MIRABELLE I'm quite sure she didn't. (*Pause*) Did she?

MARK No, but it's what she'd be thinking.

MIRABELLE It's nice of them to invite me.

MARK Well, they didn't really, did they?

MIRABELLE What?

MARK I mean I told them I was bringing you home. They didn't exactly invite you.

MIRABELLE It's nice of them to accept me then.

MARK They're probably curious. Never seen a southerner in the flesh before, you see. They probably expect you to be a little man with a briefcase and a bowler hat.

MIRABELLE You're very reassuring.

MARK It's rather like Africa really, is Padiham. The Dark Continent. With just the bright lights of Accrington twinkling on the horizon.

MIRABELLE Mark, do you remember whose idea it was that I should come and stay with you?

MARK Well...

MIRABELLE It was yours.

MARK Yes, mine.

MIRABELLE And ever since it's been arranged you've done nothing but tell me how awful it's going to be, how peculiar your parents are and how I'm not going to like them and they're not going to like me.

MARK I'm only trying to be helpful.

MIRABELLE That kind of help I can do without, thank you. I'm nervous now. And if you keep on I'm going to get more nervous.

MARK All right!

MIRABELLE It's not all right!

MARK Calm down, love, for God's sake!

MIRABELLE I am calm. I am calmly being taken to meet your parents, one of whom apparently served as a male model for Andy Capp and the other who should have been a nun but happened to get married first. Meanwhile your sister sits in a corner and knits balaclava helmets for Eskimo missionaries!

Mark laughs.

It's not bloody funny!

MARK Shhh! Keep your voice down!

MIRABELLE (*quietly*) It's not bloody funny.

MARK All right. I'm sorry, love. I'm sorry.

MIRABELLE Thank you. You might apologise to them when we get there.

MARK I just wanted to warn you that you might find things a bit different, that's all. My parents aren't like yours. I just thought I should warn you, that's all.

MIRABELLE You've never met my parents.

MARK No, but...

MIRABELLE So how can you say that yours aren't like mine?

MARK All right. Thames Ditton isn't like Padiham. Put it that way then.

MIRABELLE But no doubt there are some people in Thames Ditton who're like some people in Padiham. Put it that way.

2 The sitting room of the Baldwins' home

Sound of dance music playing. We are listening to the music of "Come Dancing" on television. A door opens.

MRS BALDWIN Here they are!

MARK (*approaching*) Hello, mum. dad.

MRS BALDWIN Hello, son! (*She kisses him.*) Turn that thing off, Jack. And how are you?

Dad turns the television off.

MARK All right, thanks.

MRS BALDWIN And this is Mirabelle, is it? Come in, love, come in!

MARK Yes. Mirabelle... er, mum and dad.

MIRABELLE Pleased to meet you.

MRS BALDWIN We've been looking forward to meeting you.

MR BALDWIN We have that. Had a good journey then, have you?

MIRABELLE I enjoyed it.

MARK We left at seven so...

MIRABELLE It was a fast train...

MR BALDWIN Well, it's good to see you both here.

MIRABELLE I hope I'm not putting you to any trouble.

MR BALDWIN No trouble at all.

MRS BALDWIN Now, come and sit down, both of you. Come

and sit by the fire. That's if you can find a space for all these newspapers.

The sound of newspapers being swept on one side.

You might put these away, Jack.

MR BALDWIN *You* were reading 'em!

MRS BALDWIN Here you are, love. Sit yourself down. You must be frozen after that train.

MIRABELLE Thank you.

MR BALDWIN I get blamed because she leaves papers lying about! What do you think about that?

MARK I'll take the cases up.

MRS BALDWIN Leave 'em there. They'll wait a minute.

MIRABELLE (*wanting an ally*) Come and sit down, Mark.

MRS BALDWIN Yes, come and get warm after that train.

MARK All right. But trains are heated, you know, mother, with doors and windows in.

MRS BALDWIN Are they now? They've improved since I last travelled in one then. Now I'll make us some tea. You'll have some tea, love?

MIRABELLE Oh yes, please. Can I help?

MRS BALDWIN (*going off*) You're not to lift a finger! I'll not be above a minute.

MR BALDWIN I suppose if she spills tea in there I'll be to blame for that!

Mirabelle laughs.

And how's college then, Mark?

MARK All right. You know . . . all right.

MR BALDWIN You stick at it. And you're . . . er . . . you're like in the same year, are you, Mirabelle?

MIRABELLE Yes. Different subject though.

MR BALDWIN Oh yes?

MIRABELLE Geography.

MR BALDWIN Geography. Capital cities and major rivers – that used to be. I daresay it's summat else now, but that's what it used to be in my day.

MARK I think you'll find there's just a bit more to it now, dad.

MIRABELLE Same capital cities and major rivers though.

MR BALDWIN Ah well, I did School Certificate, you see. That was before your O levels and your GCE's.

MARK Where's our Lynn?

MR BALDWIN Out. We see precious little of her nowadays.

She's out with John.

MARK I thought they'd be married by now.

MR BALDWIN Next year they say. They haven't fixed a date yet like. But they've been looking at a house. Mark's probably told you, Mirabelle, that he has a sister. Couple of years older than him. Engaged.

MIRABELLE Yes, Mark did say so.

MR BALDWIN Nice chap. One she's engaged to, that is. Nice chap.

MARK For a plumber.

MR BALDWIN For a plumber! Listen to him! You wouldn't be so clever if he was here. Anyway, they'll be getting wed before long.

MIRABELLE That's nice. (*Yawns*) Oh, I'm sorry!

MR BALDWIN Nay, you must be tired after that journey.

MARK Just say if you want to go to bed, Mirabelle.

MIRABELLE No, I'm all right, thanks.

MR BALDWIN And where is it you're from, Mirabelle? Mark did say, but I've forgotten.

MIRABELLE Thames Ditton, in Surrey.

MR BALDWIN Oh yes! Nice little place if my memory serves me correctly.

MARK What?

MR BALDWIN Thames Ditton. That's what you said, wasn't it, love? Thames Ditton?

MIRABELLE Yes.

MARK Don't say you know it!

MR BALDWIN Your mother and I once stopped there for lunch on a coach trip. I can't remember where we were going. Or perhaps we were coming back.

MARK Really? You stopped in Thames Ditton?

MR BALDWIN Yes. Perhaps we don't live in such a small world as you think, my lad.

MIRABELLE Where did you stop for lunch, Mr Baldwin?

MR BALDWIN Oh, I can't remember now, love. It were quite some time ago. Now, are you sure you're not feeling tired?

MIRABELLE I think perhaps I need that cup of tea more than anything.

MR BALDWIN I said you'd be in about now. Right in the middle of "Come Dancing" I said it'd be.

MARK "Come Dancing"!

MRS BALDWIN (*coming back*) Here we are then. And I've put out a bit of supper in case you were feeling peckish.

3 Bedroom (later that night)

Ticking of an alarm clock. After a few seconds, a loud crash – of a chair being knocked over. Mirabelle gives a small, startled cry.

LYNN Oh, I'm sorry,love.

MIRABELLE It's all right.

LYNN Do you mind if I put t'light on now that I've made that racket?

MIRABELLE No, not at all.

LYNN I was trying not to disturb you, you see.

She switches the lights on.

MIRABELLE I wasn't really asleep. Just lying here with my eyes closed.

LYNN You've probably guessed that I'm Lynn, Mark's sister.

MIRABELLE Yes, he told me about you. I'm Mirabelle.

LYNN Oh yes, I know that. We've had the whole house spring-cleaned on your account, so I know that. Have I left enough room for your things?

MIRABELLE I haven't unpacked yet. We've only been here for half an hour and I was so tired...

LYNN Oh, that's all right then. I'll show you tomorrow where you can use. Been going with our Mark for long, have you?

MIRABELLE Er, about four months.

LYNN Oh, that's nothing is it? I've been going out with my chap for six years.

MIRABELLE John.

LYNN Yes, John. Anyway, we're getting wed soon. Well, when I say soon I mean next year. After six years you can't pretend there's a rush, can you?

MIRABELLE A church wedding?

LYNN Oh yes! Have to be a church wedding. Not that John's a Catholic. Mind you, he said he'd turn if I asked him, but I don't think it's right somehow, do you? Not just to get married.

MIRABELLE Become a Catholic?

LYNN That's right. And mum said she didn't mind as long as it was in church. So that's what we decided on. I mean, you have to keep everybody happy, don't you?

MIRABELLE Well, it's nice if you can.

LYNN Mark's refusing to go, you know.

MIRABELLE To your wedding?

LYNN No, I mean to church. Says he's lost his faith. I said you might have lost your faith, but it doesn't cost anything to go when you're at home.

MIRABELLE Yes, he's told me.

LYNN Last time he was home he said to mum, "What would you say if I didn't go to church today?" "Oh, you'll have to go," mum said, "it's Sunday." "That's what I mean," he said. Oh, there was a right to-do! In the end mum was in tears and called him a communist!

MIRABELLE Well . . .

LYNN Oh, don't worry, love. I'm not asking you to take sides. That wouldn't be fair, would it?

4 The sitting room

Dad folds his newspaper.

MR BALDWIN Way this country's going you'll need a passport to visit Accrington in a bit.

MRS BALDWIN She's a nice girl. Don't you think so, Jack?

MR BALDWIN Who're we talking about now?

MRS BALDWIN Mirabelle, of course. A really nice girl.

MR BALDWIN Oh aye.

MRS BALDWIN I mean, she has no airs and graces. You feel she's being straight with you all the time. Made a change in our Mark too. Don't you think so, Jack?

MR BALDWIN Well, I'll say this – he's been here now for five days and I don't think we've had one word of disagreement.

MRS BALDWIN Oh, it's been wonderful.

MR BALDWIN Now if that's Mirabelle's doing then I take my hat off to that young lady, because it'd got to the stage where you couldn't express an opinion as to whether Tuesday followed Monday without him saying it didn't.

MRS BALDWIN Yes. (*Pause*) I was thinking of asking Father Drabble to call.

MR BALDWIN Father Drabble?

MRS BALDWIN Yes. Asking him to call here.

MR BALDWIN What do you want to do that for?

MRS BALDWIN For our Mark. To talk to our Mark.

MR BALDWIN I see.

MRS BALDWIN What do you think?

MR BALDWIN I don't know. What put that idea into your head?

MRS BALDWIN Well, Jack, I can't just do nothing. I can't just see my own son reject his faith and make no attempt to bring him back to it. (*Pause*) Well, can I?

MR BALDWIN No. No, it saddened me did that. It saddened me to hear him say what he did.

MRS BALDWIN Well then.

MR BALDWIN Father Drabble you think?

MRS BALDWIN Yes well, he used to know him. He's surely remember him.

MR BALDWIN Yes . . .

MRS BALDWIN And he's a clever man, you know, Jack, an educated man. The sort who can argue with our Mark. Because he will argue, you know.

MR BALDWIN Oh yes, he's argue all right. And do you think he'll come then, Father Drabble, if you ask him?

MRS BALDWIN Oh, I should think so. I mean, he must be concerned about a young man leaving the Church.

MR BALDWIN Hmmm.

MRS BALDWIN I thought I'd ask him if he could drop in on Friday afternoon. They go back on Saturday so he won't have much other chance.

MR BALDWIN And will you be there?

MRS BALDWIN No, I thought it best if I arranged to be out. You'll be at work, won't you, and I'll let our Lynn know so that she can keep out of the way.

MR BALDWIN Well, if that's what you want to do, you do it.

MRS BALDWN Nay, don't just say that, Jack.

MR BALDWIN What do you want me to say?

MRS BALDWIN Am I doing the right thing or am I not?

MR BALDWIN Yes. Yes, of course you are.

The outside door closes as Lynn comes in.

MRS BALDWIN I feel it's my duty, Jack. I can't just stand by and watch him drift away.

LYNN (*approaching*) Hello.

MRS BALDWIN Hello, love.

MR BALDWIN You been laid off then?

LYNN They let us off an hour early because boiler broke down. They'll have it fixed for tomorrow though.

MR BALDWIN Very nice. I've always wanted a job like that.

LYNN Like what?

MR BALDWIN One where you got paid for not working.

MRS BALDWIN Lynn, I want to know what you think about something.

LYNN What?

MRS BALDWIN We've been discussing something, and I'd like your opinion.

LYNN You're not trying to get me dad to buy a new suit again.

MRS BALDWIN No, this is something serious.

MR BALDWIN So was that if I remember rightly.

MRS BALDWIN It's about our Mark.

LYNN Hey, he doesn't want to get married, does he? Because she's smashing that Mirabelle, isn't she? Don't you think so, dad?

MR BALDWIN She's a very nice girl.

MRS BALDWIN No listen. It's not that.

LYNN What then?

MRS BALDWIN I thought of asking Father Drabble to call and have a word with our Mark.

LYNN Oh.

MRS BALDWIN (*pause*) Well, what do you think?

LYNN Are you going to tell Mark?

MRS BALDWIN Well, you know what he's like. I thought it'd be better if Father just seemed to call like.

LYNN And who else is going to be there?

MR BALDWIN We all have to keep out of the way.

MRS BALDWIN Yes. I thought we'd just ... leave them to it.

LYNN I see.

MRS BALDWIN (*pause*) Well, you haven't said yet what you think.

LYNN Our Mark won't like it, you know. He'll only argue with him.

MR BALDWIN Yes, we know that.

LYNN Well, don't you think you might be best ... letting sleeping dogs lie?

MRS BALDWIN Oh, Lynn; I can't ...

MR BALDWIN Your mother feels it's something she has to do.

MRS BALDWIN And you agree with me, don't you, Jack? You agree with me?

MR BALDWIN Yes, I agree with you.

LYNN Oh well then, if you've decided ...

MRS BALDWIN You think we'd be doing wrong.

LYNN I just think that you might upset things, that's all. I mean, if you want Father Drabble to call, then all right. As long as you know that things might not turn out as you want.

MR BALDWIN Things haven't turned out as we want, have they?

LYNN All right then.

MRS BALDWIN (*sighing*) I wish I knew what to do for the best.

LYNN You must decide for yourself what you want to do, mother. It's no use asking me. As I say, I'd let sleeping dogs lie, but it's not my decision.

MRS BALDWIN Well, it's what I'd like to do.

LYNN All right then.

MRS BALDWIN You won't say anything though, will you, love?

LYNN I won't say anything.

MRS BALDWIN Well, I'd feel happier to know I'd made an attempt. I don't just want things to go on as they are. I'll go and see Father Drabble tonight.

LYNN Have you finished with that paper, dad?

MR BALDWIN Yes.

He hands it to her.

MR BALDWIN I don't know why I bother. I was just saying to

your mother – way things are going you'll need a passport to visit Accrington in a bit.

LYNN So why should you want to go to Accrington?

5 The sitting room (a few days later)

MARK And what's on the cards for this afternoon then?

MIRABELLE Whatever you want.

MARK Well, I don't know really. I mean we've only this one afternoon left. I wondered if there was somewhere you particularly wanted to go.

MIRABELLE You mean we've no more relations or long-lost school friends to visit?

MARK Not that I can think of. So you can relax.

MIRABELLE Oh, I've enjoyed it. Especially your Uncle Sam with his bird imitations.

MARK God, he always does that. He used to do it when we were kids.

MIRABELLE And who was it that we went to see yesterday?

MARK Aunt Gertie.

MIRABELLE Oh yes, Aunt Gertie.

MARK Yes, I'm sorry about that.

MIRABELLE Nothing to be sorry about.

MARK Well, I'm sure you hadn't planned to spend the whole afternoon playing dominoes.

MIRABELLE No, but it made a change. (*amused*) And then she cheated! You noticed that, didn't you? She kept on cheating!

MARK Oh, she likes to win does Gertie.

They both laugh.

MARK But thanks a lot, love. It can't have been much fun.

MIRABELLE It was!

MARK Anyway, you've run the gauntlet. So what about this lovely Friday afternoon. Do you want to go for a walk?

MIRABELLE Another one?

MARK Well, there's so much to see. It could be a centre of the tourist trade could Padiham if it were handled properly. As it is, you're the first so I have to do the best I can.

MIRABELLE You haven't washed up yet.

MARK Oh, I'll do it. Don't worry.

MIRABELLE I will if you want. It's just that you said...

MARK Yes! I'm not one to welch on my washing-up commitments.

MIRABELLE I never realised you were so domesticated.

MARK Ah well...

MIRABELLE In fact a week of your mother's cooking seems to have transformed you. You've been nearly purring for the last few days.

MARK What do I normally do?

MIRABELLE I mean this dutiful son performance. After all the things you said before we came...

MARK I told you I was only joking.

MIRABELLE And they've been ever so nice!

MARU They do seem to have improved a bit.

MIRABELLE Your mother's ever so nice. I mean they've been really kind and everything.

MARK Northern hospitality.

MIRABELLE Hmm. You said that before we came, but you made it sound like a threat.

MARK Well... I didn't know how you'd get on.

MIRABELLE (*pause*) I still think that we should have offered to have gone to church with them on Sunday though.

MARK Ah no. Matter of principle was that.

MIRABELLE You didn't wake up in time you mean! They were back before you put in an appearance.

MARK That was strategy... avoiding possible confrontation.

MIRABELLE I think they went early so that we wouldn't know they were going. That was their strategy.

MARK Perhaps. You think we're a pretty nice lot then, the Baldwin family?

MIRABELLE Yes.

MARK Good.

MIRABELLE For Northerners.

MARK Give us a kiss.

MIRABELLE Washing-up?

MARK Then I'll do the washing-up (*He gives Mirabelle a quick kiss*) I suppose that's southern hospitality, is it?

MIRABELLE Oh, we might do better later.

MARK All right. (*Moving away*) I'm going! But you think we're a pretty nice lot, do you?

MIRABELLE (*amused but not insincere*) Yes, I think you're a pretty nice lot.

MARK (*going away*) She thinks we're a pretty nice lot!

LYNN (*distant*) Hey! Watch where you're going!

MARK (*distant*) Oops, sorry!

LYNN (*distant*) Dancing about like a drunken elephant!

MARK (*distant*) As one part of a pretty nice lot to another, I apologise!

LYNN (*approaching*) Has he gone daft?

MIRABELLE He's just going to do the washing-up.

LYNN Then he must have gone daft. Now listen, love, I'm just off, so I'd better say ta-ra because you're going tomorrow aren't you, and I might not see you again.

MIRABELLE Not tomorrow morning?

LYNN I'm on earlies, aren't I? Seven till three. I'll tell you what, love, you stick to your studies and get teaching. There's nowt sadder than coming in from a good night out and setting th'alarm to get you up at five-thirty. It's like signing your own death warrant.

MIRABELLE I'll remember. And thanks for everything, Lynn. You've been very kind.

LYNN Nay, it's been nice having you, love.

MIRABELLE You off to meet John?

LYNN (*pleased*) Do I look like it?

MIRABELLE You look lovely.

LYNN Thanks. I'm sorry you haven't met him, love. I really am. Perhaps next time, eh?

MIRABELLE Yes. Anyway, the best of luck.

LYNN Thanks. And to you, love. (*Pause*) Mum and dad do like you, you know.

MIRABELLE They're very nice.

LYNN And they aren't half pleased with the way you've changed our Mark!

MIRABELLE Changed him?

LYNN 'Course you won't know what it had got like before. When he came home from college last year it were rows all the time.

MIRABELLE What about?

LYNN Church . . .

MIRABELLE Oh.

LYNN Half the time anyway. And then he never seemed content until he'd gone back again. Always on edge, you know. As if he didn't like coming home.

MIRABELLE He's never said anything.

LYNN Oh, don't worry about it, love. You've got him washing-up. Let's leave it at that.

MIRABELLE I don't know that I deserve the credit.

LYNN Well, you're getting it whether you deserve it or not. Now I've got to dash. I'll get me head bitten off if I'm late. Is me mam out?

MIRABELLE She went out half on hour ago.

LYNN Oh. (*pause*) You know she's still worried about Mark . . . and Church and things.

MIRABELLE I thought she might be.

LYNN Has she said anything to you?

MIRABELLE What about?

LYNN Well, about it.

MIRABELLE Oh no.

LYNN Ah well, you mustn't be surprised if . . . well, at whatever she might do . . .

MIRABELLE She might do?

LYNN She might do to try and persuade him back.

MIRABELLE Oh. What . . . what sort of thing might she do?

LYNN Well . . .

The door bell rings.

Oh, listen to that! There's somebody at our door.

MIRABELLE It might be your mother. Forgotten her key or something.

LYNN No, I don't think it'd be her. Look, love, I'll get killed if I'm late. Do you mind if I slip out . . . ?

MIRABELLE No, of course not. You go, Lynn, and have a good time.

LYNN Ta, love, you're a good 'un. I'll slip out the back door.

MIRABELLE I'll see who it is.

LYNN (*going away*) And don't worry about it, love!

MIRABELLE Bye, Lynn! (*To herself, puzzled*) Don't worry about what?

We hear the sound of a front door being opened. Perhaps the background sound of distant traffic.

Oh!

FATHER D Good afternoon.

MIRABELLE Good afternoon.

FATHER D I was wondering if Mark Baldwin was at home.

MIRABELLE Mark?

FATHER D Yes.

MIRABELLE Oh yes. Yes, he is.

FATHER D Could I possibly . . . ?

MIRABELLE Would you like to come in?

FATHER D Thank you.

The door is closed.

I have managed to catch him then?

MIRABELLE Oh yes, he's doing . . . He's in the kitchen. Would you like to sit down? I'll tell him you're here . . . Father.

6 The kitchen

MARK Are you having me on?

MIRABELLE (*speaking quietly, aware of the visitor next door*) No!

MARK A priest?

MIRABELLE Yes. In the living room.

MARK What's his name?

MIRABELLE I didn't ask. He just said he wanted to speak to you.

MARK I might have known it was too good to be true.

MIRABELLE What?

MARK The truce, the one that seems to have been in operation this week. Having lulled us into a false sense of security, they're now gathering for the attack.

MIRABELLE There's only one of him.

MARK Ah, but he has God on his side!

MIRABELLE Don't be silly, Mark. You've no idea why he's here.

MARK I have a very good idea why he's here.

MIRABELLE And you might be wrong. Now, are you coming in, or what?

MARK Yes! See what cunning strategies they've concocted.

MIRABELLE Then take your apron off first, won't you?

Fade out to show passage of time.

FATHER D I don't honestly know that I'd have recognised you. It must be all of... what, seven years?

MARK Six or seven.

FATHER D Well, it's very nice to see you again.

MARK Yes.

FATHER D And this is, er...?

MARK Oh, Mirabelle. Sorry. Mirabelle, this is Father Drabble.

FATHER D Hello, Mirabelle.

MIRABELLE Hello, Father.

FATHER D You're both at college together, I believe?

MIRABELLE Yes.

MARK (*with a touch of hostility*) My mother told you I suppose.

FATHER D Yes... yes, I suppose she must have done.

MIRABELLE We've been up here for the week and go back tomorrow.

FATHER D A taste of home comforts?

MIRABELLE Something like that.

MARK We live together actually.

MIRABELLE (*gently*) Mark!

MARK I mean when we're at college. We share a flat.

FATHER D (*unperturbed*) Very nice. And how is college? Everything going well?

MARK It's all right.

FATHER D You're in your second year?

MARK Yes.

MIRABELLE (*pause*) Can I get us some coffee? Father Drabble, would you like some coffee?

FATHER D It would be nice, thank you.

MIRABELLE Mark?

MARK I don't want any.

MIRABELLE Right.

MARK Are you sure you can find everything?

MIRABELLE Quite sure, thank you.

MARK Oh, go on then. I'll have one. Please.

MIRABELLE (*moving away*) Three coffees.

There is a short pause.

FATHER D I'd heard that you were home.

MARK From my mother?

FATHER D Yes, from your mother. It was she who suggested that I called actually.

MARK I thought it might be.

FATHER D Well, there's no point in beating about the bush, is there? I mean, I'm very glad to meet you again, delighted to meet . . . er . . .

MARK Mirabelle.

FATHER D Mirabelle. But there's no point in pretending. I'm sure we both know that the main reason I'm here is that your mother asked me to call and see you.

MARK And we know why.

FATHER D She's very upset because you've said to her that you've left the Church.

MARK I have left the Church.

FATHER D Yes.

MARK I mean, I haven't just said so. I've done it.

FATHER Yes . . . Er . . . what have you done exactly?

MARK What have I done?

FATHER D I just wondered what counted as formally leaving. What you had to do. I mean, there's no way of physically walking out because there's nowhere to physically walk out of. And there's no membership card to tear up.

MARK I don't go to Church any more. And I don't believe.

FATHER D You don't believe in the Church?

MARK I don't believe in God. Or in any of it.

FATHER D Hmm. Well, I can't say I blame you.

MARK (*pause*) You don't blame me? Don't tell me you're an atheist as well?

FATHER D No, I'm a priest.

MARK Then how can you say that there's nothing wrong with being an atheist?

FATHER D Oh, I didn't say that. I said I wouldn't blame you for it. What I mean is that if I were in your position then I'd probably hold much the same views.

MARK You'd be an atheist?

FATHER D No doubt a fairly fervent one. You've probably noticed I tend to carry my beliefs to extremes.

MARK I still don't see...

FATHER D All that I'm saying really is that if I'd been born in nineteen-fifty-whatever-it-was and was living with a lovely girl in London then I'd probably have no more time for religion than you have.

MARK Oh, I see.

FATHER D Good.

MARK At least I think I see. What you might call the individual consciousness determined by social forces approach.

FATHER D You could put it like that.

MARK That's almost Marxist.

FATHER D Yes! I suppose it is.

MARK And does it work the other way round? If I'm an atheist only because of my background, are you a priest only because of yours?

FATHER D Well, that's a bit too simple. Let's say that there was nothing in my background to stop me becoming a priest.

MARK Don't tell me that it runs in the family – your father was a priest before you!

FATHER D (*amused*) No, no, I wasn't going to claim that.

MARK What then?

FATHER D Well, I was educated in a convent. That must have helped. I don't think I ever met a non-Catholic – as we patronisingly called them – until my late teens. And that was at Oxford so it was a fairly High Anglican variety even then!

MARK So you might say that you were conned into it really?

FATHER D If, by the same token, you would say that you were conned out of it.

MARK (*pause*) But you don't mind? I mean that I don't go to Church and things. You don't mind that?

FATHER D I mind very much. That's why I'm here.

MARK Hmm. What about – to take another example of my erroneous ways – what about the fact that I live with Mirabelle?

FATHER D What about it?

MARK Well, I've told you I live with her. We live together.

FATHER D What would you like me to do?

MARK You don't mind about that either?

FATHER D It's not a question of whether I mind or not...

MARK I thought it was called living in sin.

FATHER D It is.

MARK So would you say that we're committing mortal sin when we sleep together?

FATHER D Would you like me to say it? Would you like me to condemn you to eternal damnation? I know you wouldn't believe me if I did, but would you like me to for form's sake?

MARK All I want to know is are we or are we not committing mortal sin when we sleep together?

Pause, Mirabelle enters.

MIRABELLE (*approaching*) Coffee!

FATHER D Ah, thank you.

MARK Huh!

MIRABELLE Take any one.

MARK Are we or are we not committing mortal sin when we sleep together?

FATHER D Yes!

MARK Well, that's a relief.

FATHER D Technically.

Mark sighs in despair.

MIRABELLE Am I... interrupting something?

FATHER D I think your boyfriend was about to confess to me.

MARK I was not!

FATHER D Hmm, nice coffee.

MIRABELLE Thank you.

MARK I was trying to get Father Drabble to commit himself to something.

MIRABELLE Oh.

MARK Apart from liking your coffee, he seems unwilling to admit to anything.

FATHER D Now that's not quite fair. Most people might feel that the way that I dress alone commits me to a good deal.

MIRABELLE Would you like me to leave so that you can talk?

MARK Well...

FATHER D Please don't leave for my sake, Mirabelle.

MARK I don't know that we've much to talk about.

MIRABELLE Oh well, I'd rather stay.

FATHER D Then do.

MIRABELLE But I'd better warn you – I'm not much good at religion.

FATHER D Neither am I. At least not in fulfilling the role that Mark seems to expect of me.

MARK And what role's that?

FATHER D A sort of shepherd seeking lost sheep, I think.

MIRABELLE And Mark's the sheep?

FATHER D Well, no. That's the trouble.

MIRABELLE Oh, I see.

MARK You want a smoke?

MIRABELLE Yes please.

MARK Do you smoke, Father?

FATHER D No, I won't, thank you. But don't worry – I don't regard it as a sin.

MARK I didn't think you would.

A pause whilst they light cigarettes.

FATHER D Are you a Christian, Mirabelle?

MIRABELLE Well, I suppose I'm labelled Church of England, but I don't know that it means much.

FATHER D You haven't left then?

MIRABELLE No. But I don't really go either. To be honest, I don't really think about it much.

FATHER D (*amused*) Your Church does have the virtue of serenity. You don't seem to suffer all the emotional hang-ups that we get ourselves into.

MIRABELLE Mark's the first Catholic I've really known.

FATHER D Oh, we're all the same.

MARK Except I'm not a Catholic.

FATHER D No, of course not.

MARK Father Drabble's been sent by mother.

MIRABELLE Oh.

MARK He's been charged with the task of converting me back to the true faith.

FATHER D Your mother did suggest that I might like to call and talk to you.

MARK And why?

FATHER D Well yes. I'm sure she hoped that I might be able to help in some way.

MARK She didn't tell us anything about this, you know.

FATHER D Well, does that matter very much one way or the other?

MARK Yes.

MIRABELLE Oh, Mark, don't be silly. It's very nice to meet Father Drabble. Did you used to teach Mark or...?

FATHER D No, I'm the parish priest here. I don't really teach any more apart from confirmation classes at the junior school. Though I suppose I must have once taught you in one of those, Mark. I've been doing them for more years than I care to remember.

MARK I suppose so.

FATHER D No, I really got to know Mark when he was on the altar.

MIRABELLE On the altar?

FATHER D He used to be an altar-boy. Wore a cassock and used to assist at various services. Quite angelic he was really. At least I thought so until I once caught him smoking in the sacristy.

MARK Oh yes, I'd forgotten about that!

MIRABELLE You never told me you were an altar – what? – an altar-boy.

MARK I do have a few guilty secrets.

FATHER D He'd have been head altar-boy if he'd stayed on another year.

MIRABELLE Well, well, well!

MARK I'm just not the ambitious kind. (*Pause*) Look, I don't want to be rude, Father, but you're really wasting your time, you know.

FATHER D Oh, I wouldn't say that.

MARK I would. I've left the Church. I've no intention of going back and I can't see that anything you might say is going to make the slightest difference.

FATHER D Would you believe that I left the Church once?

MARK (*amused despite himself*) You didn't make a very good job of it!

FATHER D No, I suppose I didn't. But I didn't start wearing my collar like this until I was thirty, you know. When I was your age, er... twenty-three?

MARK Twenty-one.

FATHER D Twenty-one, I didn't believe in God either.

MARK Comforting to know that it was only a temporary lapse.

FATHER D Yes, but – it's the point I was making before – if my circumstances had been different then so might the outcome have been.

MARK In the great, wide world of the atheistic eighties ...

FATHER D You could say that. As it was, I spent my two years as an atheist working in a library, the reference section, and walking out with a young lady from the Legion of Mary every Sunday afternoon and on Tuesday evenings after Novenas. Never stood a chance really.

MIRABELLE What's Novenas, please?

MARK It's a service. A Novena. A kind of service.

MIRABELLE Oh. And what happened to the young lady?

FATHER D Do you know, I've no idea.

MIRABELLE Sad really.

FATHER D Oh, I daresay she's got over it by now.

MARK So it's all a question of environment then?

FATHER D I think... some of it is.

MARK So if you made the Pope manager of Crystal Palace he'd be the playboy of the western world before the season was over?

FATHER D Possibly... and it might not do Crystal Palace any harm either.

MIRABELLE Crystal Palace, the football team?

MARK Yes. And you know who the Pope is, don't you?

MIRABELLE Yes, thank you.

FATHER D No, obviously it's not as simple as that. God could make any man his own no matter who or what that man was. But if everything about a man's life and the world he lives in tells him that there is no God, then it's a rare man who can keep his faith alive.

MARK Oh, come on, Father, this is too much!

FATHER D What is?

MARK We're sitting here, drinking coffee, agreeing over everything. For God's sake, I'm an atheist and you're a priest!

MIRABELLE That doesn't mean you have to argue.

MARK It does if we're going to talk about religion. And that's what he's here for.

FATHER D I wouldn't say . . .

MARK Unless you're here just to keep my mother happy.

FATHER D If that were a reason it wouldn't be a bad one, would it?

MIRABELLE I think it's a good reason.

MARK I think it's a bloody stupid reason!

FATHER D It is a reason though.

MARK And what will you tell her? That you've failed to drag me from the jaws of hell?

FATHER D I'll tell her that you seem very happy – for an atheist – and that she isn't to worry about you.

MARK Thank you. The Church's modern approach is this, is it?

FATHER D What?

MARK You don't condemn the sinner – you patronise him. Make him feel small-minded or something.

FATHER D My dear Mark, for a self-confessed atheist, you seem intent on being condemned for your sins.

MIRABELLE I've told him that.

FATHER D Really?

MARK You've told me what?

MIRABELLE For an atheist you're always talking about religion.

MARK I am not always talking about religion.

MIRABELLE He's always talking about it. Gets into arguments at parties.

MARK All right then. I am always talking about religion. I never talk about anything else. I talk about religion in my sleep.

MIRABELLE Now you're being silly.

MARK Well, I even talk about religion when I'm silly.

MIRABELLE That's certainly true.

MARK So you'll tell mummy everything's all right, will you, Father? Keep taking the tablets and there's nothing to worry about.

FATHER D Well, I don't think there is. Do you?

MARK Oh, it's not what I say that matters. She won't take any notice of that.

MIRABELLE Why do you say that?

MARK It's what Father Drabble says that matters.

FATHER D Yes.

MARK I mean it.

FATHER D So do I. That's what makes this job difficult. Not the people like you who won't believe, but the people like your mother who believes everything.

MARK Some ego-trip though.

FATHER D Some . . .?

MARK For you.

FATHER D Oh, I see.

MIRABELLE That's another thing he's an expert on – ego-trips.

MARK Well, it must be. All these females looking for guidance.

FATHER D Oh, it's there at first. True enough. Vocations and ego-trips often get confused for one another. But you soon get over it. You soon find that, anyway, it's not you that people are interested in. It's just the priest. Even if they know your name they won't use it. Just Father.

MARK Yes, Father.

FATHER D Stuart.

MARK Pardon?

FATHER D That's my name. Stuart.

MARK Oh.

MIRABELLE Would you like some more coffee, Stuart?

FATHER D Well, Mirabelle, I think perhaps I've kept you long enough as it is.

MIRABELLE I'm having some more anyway. And we're not going anywhere, are we, Mark?

MARK It doesn't look like it.

MIRABELLE So you'll have some, Stuart?

FATHER D If you don't mind. Yes please.

MIRABELLE Mark?

MARK No.

MIRABELLE (*going away*) Suit yourself.

Mirabelle goes. There is a pause.

FATHER D You don't have any belief in any kind of God at all, Mark?

MARK Not a shred. (*Pause*) You do believe in God I suppose?

FATHER D Oh yes. Be silly if I didn't.

MARK I was beginning to wonder. You seem pretty casual about it.

FATHER D I think that's probably just my bedside manner. But I believe all right if that's what's worrying you.

MARK In what?

FATHER D In what?

MARK Well, in who then? This God of yours, what sort of God is he?

FATHER D That's difficult.

MARK Really.

FATHER D You want me to describe him, do you? You won't be content if I just say The Supreme Being or something like that?

MARK No.

FATHER D I didn't think you would. You want to know precisely and in detail what I mean when I say I believe in God?

MARK Yes.

FATHER D Hmm?

MARK I mean it's easy for my mother. No problems at all for her.

FATHER D You really think so?

MARK I'm sure! For her God is an old man with a long, white beard who sits up there in heaven thrilled to bits when she fawns all over him on a Sunday morning and furious with me when I don't.

FATHER D Hmm . . . I recognise the picture. Though the way that people talk about God and the way that they experience him can be very different things.

MARK No, that's how she sees him. You ask her.

FATHER D I . . . probably won't.

Mirabelle comes back.

MIRABELLE (*approaching*) Coffee again!

FATHER D Thank you, Mirabelle.

MIRABELLE Am I interrupting again?

FATHER D Oh no. Your timing was perfect.

MARK We were talking about images of God. The way that my mother's differs from Father Drabble's here.

FATHER D We didn't say that, did we?

MARK It's true though, isn't it?

MIRABELLE What do you mean? Sorry, I'm not . . .

FATHER D Mark was suggesting that his mother sees God as a sort of old man in the sky.

MIRABELLE Oh.

MARK Look, they have a statue of Christ in church – haven't you, Father? – the big one in front of the altar.

FATHER D Yes.

MARK And it's a dead ringer for Bryan Robson.

Mirabelle laughs.

FATHER D (*also amused*) It is . . . er . . . similar.

MARK From ten yards you couldn't tell them apart. Anyway, I said to my mother – in one of our little religious discussions that we have from time to time – I said, why have you got a statue of Bryan Robson in front of the altar?

MIRABELLE That's a discussion?

MARK Yes.

MIRABELLE It sounds like one.

MARK Well, of course, she said, it's a statue of Jesus. And I said, do you mean that that's what Jesus looked like? And she said, yes. And so I said, have you seen pictures of those Palestinian guerillas? You know, the Palestinian Liberation movement people? Well, that's what Jesus looked like if he looked like anything – a Palestinian terrorist.

MIRABELLE And she said?

MARK Oh, she said it was blasphemy.

FATHER D (*amused*) Blasphemy!?

MARK Yes, and that's what I mean, see? In her eyes, and she's not the only one, God is white, male and Caucasian. And probably votes Conservative.

FATHER D Well, I suppose he's as much that as he is anything else. Don't you think it's all a bit superficial though?

MARK What?

FATHER D Not really important... what image you use.

MARK What image do you use then?

FATHER D I thought I'd already avoided that question.

MARK You agree with mummy and her cronies? God as a vain, old man who wants worshipping all the time?

FATHER D (*sighs heavily, reluctant to be pushed to an answer*) Everybody has to simplify...

MARK Do you agree with them or not?

FATHER D I wouldn't describe my image of God in those terms.

MARK So the answer's no?

FATHER D (*carefully*) The answer is neither yes nor no. I might share much of what the image stands for, but not altogether the image itself.

MARK I don't suppose you ever tell them this.

FATHER D Tell them what?

MIRABELLE Mark, that's not very fair.

MARK I just want to know, that's all! I don't see what's unfair about it.

MIRABELLE Well, I don't think it's very fair.

FATHER D You mean do I tell my parishioners that our images of God may not be quite identical?

MARK Yes. Do you tell them that you don't believe what they believe?

The distant sound of a door being opened and closed.

MIRABELLE Someone's come in!

FATHER D That wasn't what I said.

MARK It's what it amounted to. Either you see Christ as Bryan Robson or you don't. There are no two ways about it.

MRS BALDWIN (*approaching*) Good afternoon, Father.

FATHER D Mrs Baldwin! How nice to see you.

MARK (*ominously*) Hello, mother.

MRS BALDWIN Are they looking after you all right, Father? Can I get you anything?

FATHER D Mirabelle's been supplying me with coffee, thank you.

MRS BALDWIN Good girl.

MIRABELLE No trouble.

MARK Have you come to lend weight to the attack then, mother?

MRS BALDWIN Pardon, Mark?

MARK You know what I mean.

MIRABELLE Can I get you some coffee or something, Mrs Baldwin?

MRS BALDWIN No, thank you love. Nothing for me. Would you like me to leave you, Father, if you're... talking?

FATHER D Oh, we're just exchanging views. It's very nice to see Mark again.

MRS BALDWIN Well, it's nice of you to call, Father.

MARK Not exactly chance though, was it?

MRS BALDWIN Pardon, Mark?

MARK Father Drabble calling. Not exactly chance.

MRS BALDWIN I don't know what you're insinuating...

FATHER D I told Mark that you'd been to see me and that we'd agreed I might call.

MRS BALDWIN Oh yes...

MIRABELLE We've had a very interesting talk, haven't we, Stuart?

MRS BALDWIN Mirabelle!

MIRABELLE Pardon?

MRS BALDWIN This is Father Drabble. You must address him as Father.

FATHER D Oh, that's not necessary, really Mrs Baldwin.

MARK Anyway, I'm afraid I'm not rejoining the flock, mother. So you can send the fatted calf back to the butchers.

MRS BALDWIN Now, Mark. Father Drabble's taken the trouble to call. The least you can do is listen to what he's got to say.

MARK I listened! Didn't I listen?

FATHER D You listened. He did listen.

MRS BALDWIN Well then, I can only hope that you've come to your senses, Mark, after hearing what Father has to say.

MARK I haven't lost my senses, mother. You're as bad as the bloody Russians!

MRS BALDWIN Language!

MARK (*patiently*) You're as bad as the Russians.

MRS BALDWIN I'm sure I don't know what the Russians have to do with this.

MARK They share your tendency for attributing insanity to anyone who disagrees with them.

MRS BALDWIN Disagrees with them about what?

MARK Politics. Anything.

MRS BALDWIN We're not talking about politics, dear. You know very well what we're talking about.

MARK (*mutters*) Bryan Robson.

MRS BALDWIN What?

MARK Nothing, nothing.

FATHER D You know, Mrs Baldwin, there's always one thing to be said about people who leave the Church for a time. And that is that they are at least thinking about their religion. After all, it's easy enough to go through life being a Catholic and never really stopping to think what that means.

MRS BALDWIN (*pause*) I hope you don't feel your time's been wasted, Father.

FATHER D Not at all! I've had the pleasure of meeting Mirabelle for one thing.

MRS BALDWIN Mirabelle's a lovely girl. (*Suddenly dangerously close to tears*) You mustn't think I hold it against you, Mirabelle, love. I mean, you not being a Catholic.

MIRABELLE Oh no! I've never thought anything like that.

MRS BALDWIN It's just that we've always been a Catholic family . . .

MIRABELLE Yes, of course.

MRS BALDWIN Mark was brought up a Catholic, you see . . .

FATHER D Mrs Baldwin . . .

MRS BALDWIN Where did I go wrong, Father? It must have been my fault somewhere . . .

FATHER D I'm sure it's not a matter of anybody's being at fault.

MARK Oh, God!

MRS BALDWIN (*bitterly*) And thou shalt not take the name of the Lord Thy God in vain!

MARK It's not my God!

MIRABELLE Mark!

MARK Well, it's just blackmail is this! Either I go to church or my mother's miserable and it's my fault. It's just emotional bloody blackmail!

MRS BALDWIN There's no need to take my feelings into account...

FATHER D Mrs Baldwin, please try and remain calm...

MRS BALDWIN He has denied God, Father! I find it difficult to remain calm when I hear my own son deny God!

MARK Deny God! (*He laughs*)

MRS BALDWIN Listen to him now! He mocks God and he mocks me!

MARK I am not mocking you, mother. And I daresay that your God is a lot more thick-skinned than you make him out to be.

MRS BALDWIN Listen to that, Father!

MARK And it so happens that Father Drabble agrees with me!

FATHER D (*pause*) Now, Mark, you have no right to say that.

MARK Oh, come on, Father! You're not going to deny what you said a minute ago?

FATHER D I won't deny anything I actually did say...

MARK Then didn't you say that the God you believe in isn't the same as the God that my mother believes in?

FATHER D In those words, no!

MARK In any words?

MRS BALDWIN Mark!

MARK What?

MRS BALDWIN I asked Father Drabble to call...

MARK Yes.

MRS BALDWIN And I'm not having you talk to him like that!

MARK It doesn't occur to you that I might be telling the truth?

MRS BALDWIN What could be true about a ridiculous statement like that?

FATHER D Perhaps I should...

MARK Everything! He doesn't even believe in your sort of God!

FATHER D Perhaps, Mark, if you'd allow me, I should explain what it was we were talking about.

MIRABELLE No, Stuart, I don't think you should.

MARK And why not?

MIRABELLE I don't think he should have to explain himself.

MRS BALDWIN Well, I'm sure I don't know who's said what anymore. Perhaps it'd be best if I went.

FATHER D It's really nothing to worry about, Mrs Baldwin. We were talking about belief in God and, well, the different ways in which people think of him.

MARK The very different ways.

MRS BALDWIN Oh.

FATHER D For example, not everybody sees God as a person.

MARK Or as Bryan Robson.

MIRABELLE Shut up, Mark!

MRS BALDWIN (*unconvinced*) I see.

FATHER D (*severely*) But that, young man, is not the same as saying that I am in any way on your side!

MRS BALDWIN Perhaps I shouldn't have come at all, should I? Perhaps I don't understand these things at all.

MIRABELLE (*attempting a laugh*) I'm sure I don't!

MRS BALDWIN I shall go upstairs. If you'll excuse me, Father, I shall go upstairs so that you can talk about whatever it is you want to talk about.

MIRABELLE Mark!

MARK What?

MIRABELLE Tell your mother not to leave.

MARK (*flatly*) Mother, don't leave.

MRS BALDWIN I'm sorry if I've said the wrong things, Father. You see, I haven't had the education that you've all had. I suppose that's the difference, isn't it?

FATHER D Mrs Baldwin, please...

MIRABELLE Don't go!

MRS BALDWIN (*going away*) You must forgive an old woman for her silly, old-fashioned beliefs.

She goes upstairs.

MIRABELLE Oh no.

MARK Well, we told her to stay.

FATHER D I told you faith was a fragile thing. Easily shattered.

MARK You're not telling me she doesn't believe in God now!

FATHER D I mean her faith in me.

MARK Oh, well, I'm sorry about that, but, well, you did say it.

FATHER D I did not. Anyway, that's beside the point now. The real pity is that before your mother arrived you were just beginning to show how religious you really are.

MARK Religious!

FATHER D Yes.

MIRABELLE But thoughtless with it.

MARK And what's that supposed to mean?

MIRABELLE Never mind.

MARK I can't see why everybody has to be so bloody careful about everybody else's beliefs but mine! I'm supposed to feel guilty as hell if I don't happen to agree with my mother, the Pope and their lot, but it's all right for them to accuse me of being insincere, dishonest and anything else they care to throw in.

FATHER D Yes. Yes, I'm sure you're right.

MARK Ha!

FATHER D If it's any consolation.

MARK You might have said that before.

FATHER D I suppose I might. But now, if it doesn't look too much like escaping from the scene of the crime, I must be going. It's very nice to have met you both.

MIRABELLE Nice to have met you, Stuart.

FATHER D I hope we'll meet again. But in the meantime you be kind to your mother, young man...

7 The kitchen (next day)

The occasional rattle of breakfast things.

MR BALDWIN What time are they off then?

MRS BALDWIN I don't know exactly. Sometime this morning.

MR BALDWIN Hadn't you better give 'em a call?

MRS BALDWIN No, they're up. I've heard 'em stirring. Would you like some bacon, Jack? I'm doing some for them so it'd be no trouble.

MR BALDWIN No, thank you. But what I would like, before they come down, is to be told exactly what happened yesterday afternoon.

MRS BALDWIN Oh, Jack. I've already told you.

MR BALDWIN You've told me nothing right.

MRS BALDWIN We had an argument. I came in and we had an argument.

MR BALDWIN I thought you weren't going to be there?

MRS BALDWIN No. (*Pause*) I wasn't but... Well, I went across to Elsie's and...

MR BALDWIN And then you got nosey. All right. But what was the argument about?

MRS BALDWIN Well, our Mark was saying some things about God – things I'm not going to repeat...

MR BALDWIN I can imagine.

MRS BALDWIN I should have kept out of the way, shouldn't I?

MR BALDWIN Well, you might have left it to Father Drabble. That was what you got him here for.

MRS BALDWIN Well yes, but... I know it sounds silly, but I got the impression that he agreed with our Mark more than he agreed with me.

MR BALDWIN Agreed with our Mark!

MRS BALDWIN Oh, I suppose it was just me. I got so confused that after five minutes I couldn't make head nor tail of who was saying what.

MR BALDWIN Well, I'm sure I don't know.

MRS BALDWIN The thing is... I feel a bit funny about seeing Father Drabble again.

MR BALDWIN Oh, he'll be used to that sort of thing.

MRS BALDWIN No, it's not that. I mean I don't feel that I trust him any more.

MR BALDWIN Perhaps we should have listened to our Lynn. She was against the whole idea and perhaps she was right. Anyhow, would you like me to have a word with that young man of ours before he goes?

MRS BALDWIN Oh no, Jack. Please. You'll only start him off again.

MR BALDWIN He won't start off anything with me.

We hear the faint sound of feet descending stairs.

MRS BALDWIN Anyway, they're coming down now.

MR BALDWIN I said before they came in that I wasn't having him upsetting you again.

MRS BALDWIN Now, Jack, please!

Mark and Mirabelle come in.

MARK (*approaching*) Good morning.

MIRABELLE (*approaching*) Good morning, Mr Baldwin. Good morning, Mrs Baldwin.

MR BALDWIN Morning.

MRS BALDWIN Sit yourselves down there. Now, Mirabelle, would you like a fried tomato with your egg and bacon?

MIRABELLE Oh no thank you, Mrs Baldwin. Actually I was wondering if I could just have some toast.

MRS BALDWIN Well, I've already made it.

MIRABELLE Oh, that's all right then.

MRS BALDWIN I thought you'd want a hot breakfast before travelling.

MIRABELLE Oh, egg and bacon's fine, thanks. I just... didn't know that you'd made it.

MRS BALDWIN You'll be glad of it later, I'm sure.

MARK I wouldn't mind a fried tomato please. (*Pause*) I wouldn't mind a fried tomato please.

MR BALDWIN Your mother heard you the first time!

MARK Oh, only she didn't say anything.

MR BALDWIN I thought that's what you preferred. That she shouldn't say anything.

MRS BALDWIN Now, Jack...

MARK I simply said that I wouldn't mind a fried tomato. Since nobody answered I was thus left in some suspense as to whether my egg and bacon would arrive with the aforementioned fried tomato or without the aforementioned fried tomato.

MR BALDWIN I'm going to work! (*He moves from the table*) I'll swing for this character if I have to take any more of his cleverness!

MRS BALDWIN Nay, Jack, you're not leaving your breakfast half finished?

MR BALDWIN I am that. I'd leave a four-course dinner before I'd have to listen to any more of his cheek.

MARK What have I done all of a sudden?

MR BALDWIN I'll say goodbye then, Mirabelle. It's been a real pleasure to have you here. I just hope that this... this little affair that we had yesterday hasn't spoiled things too much for you.

MIRABELLE Thank you, Mr Baldwin. It's been lovely meeting you all and everything.

MARK I only said that I wouldn't mind a fried tomato ...

MR BALDWIN Give him a bloody tomato! Give him two bloody tomatoes and let him take 'em back with him and share 'em with his bloody communist friends!

The door is slammed loudly as Mr Baldwin leaves. There is a pause.

MRS BALDWIN Now look what you've done.

MARK Perhaps I won't bother with a tomato after all, thank you.

MRS BALDWIN There we are, Mirabelle.

She puts the plate down.

MIRABELLE Thank you.

MRS BALDWIN Would you like a piece of fried bread? It wouldn't take a minute.

MIRABELLE Er... no... thank you.

MRS BALDWIN I'll make some coffee. What time did you say your train was?

MIRABELLE Half past ten is it, Mark?

MARK Ten thirty-seven.

MRS BALDWIN It'll be soon enough for you I daresay. Soon enough to get back. I'm sure that this part of the world can't have much to offer you any more...

8 A train carriage

Sound of a high-speed train. This is held for a moment, then faded into background.

MARK Cigarette?

MIRABELLE No thank you.

Pause, Mark lights a cigarette.

MARK What's the matter, love?

MIRABELLE What?

MARK You know.

MIRABELLE You want to know what's the matter because I don't want a cigarette?

MARK I want to know what's the matter because we've been sitting here for half an hour like a couple of complete strangers.

MIRABELLE I've been thinking.

MARK About yesterday.

MIRABELLE Yes. About yesterday.

MARK So you're annoyed... I can take it that you're annoyed, can I?

MIRABELLE Yes.

MARK Right. So you're annoyed because of what I said yesterday to my mother and to Father What's-his-name?

MIRABELLE You know his name.

MARK Father Drabble. Or Stuart to his friends.

MIRABELLE Yes.

MARK Well, they started it, you know. I was quite happy to leave things as they were.

MIRABELLE You haven't left anything as it was.

MARK They started all the aggro.

MIRABELLE And weren't you pleased?

MARK What?

MIRABELLE It was just what you were waiting for, wasn't it? A chance to really stick the boot in!

MARK Oh, thank you.

MIRABELLE And I'll have that cigarette now please.

MARK I was perfectly happy with things as they were. Then they had to start. I should have known all along that it was too good to be true.

Mark lights her cigarette.

MIRABELLE You must have been getting disappointed.

MARK About what?

MIRABELLE Because everything was nice and ordinary, just nice and ordinary.

MARK I never said it'd be anything else.

MIRABELLE Oh no!

MARK Well, what did I say?

MIRABELLE That your family were a gang of religious freaks living on the very edge of civilisation.

MARK I never said that.

MIRABELLE You know what I mean. All the little jokes – no, my family don't have a telephone; if they had, they might try and keep coal in it.

MARK It was only a joke. They don't use coal for one thing.

MIRABELLE (*pause*) For the record I thought your performance yesterday afternoon was disgusting.

MARK Oh. (*Pause*) Well, I'm sorry about that.

MIRABELLE Well, I did.

MARK Because I was wrong?

MIRABELLE No. I don't know whether you were right or wrong. Just bloody unkind.

MARK Unkind.

MIRABELLE Yes, to your mother.

MARK I see.

MIRABELLE And unfair to Father Drabble. Anybody could see he'd only come round to keep your mother happy. But he was just ammunition as far as you were concerned.

MARK Come on! That religious gentleman is a very smooth operator. It was like trying to argue with a snake.

MIRABELLE He wasn't there to argue.

MARK He was there to argue all right. But not so's that you'd notice. Not so's that you could get to grips with him.

MIRABELLE So you got annoyed and took it out on your mother!

MARK I did not get annoyed or take anything out on my mother. Though God knows what she thought she was doing walking in like that. (*Pause*) Come on, love. Let's be friends again.

MIRABELLE Oh, for God's sake!

MARK Well, you can't keep this up for ever. I mean, all right, we had a miserable night last night, we had a miserable breakfast this morning, we're having a miserable train journey now . . . Well, how much longer is it going to go on?

MIRABELLE I haven't decided yet.

MARK Oh. You mean . . .

MIRABELLE I haven't decided yet.

MARK (*with rising anger*) You mean you want us to finish? Just because of that stupid bloody row you want us to finish?

MIRABELLE Keep your voice down.

MARK (*quietly*) Is that what you mean?

MIRABELLE I don't know. I've told you I don't know.

MARK I see. This week's little insights have shown you just how vindictive and evil I really am.

MIRABELLE You aren't vindictive and evil.

MARK Oh, thank you.

MIRABELLE Just . . . oh, I don't know . . . single-minded. You want to show everybody how wrong they are.

MARK I'm sorry you see things like that.

MIRABELLE Don't apologise to me.

MARK Well, I'm not sorry then. That is, I am sorry, but I won't say I'm sorry. (*Pause*) Come on, love, give us another chance. It's not the end of the world, you know.

MIRABELLE You can't just . . . keep quiet and let everybody lead a happy life?

MARK I haven't noticed other people keeping quiet so that I can lead a happy life.

MIRABELLE Oh, be fair. You know your parents are never going to change. Okay, why not just leave it?

MARK (*spelling it out*) I didn't start it!

MIRABELLE They're only worried about you.

MARK About me? Or about my immortal soul?

MIRABELLE I suspect it's you.

MARK Huh.

MIRABELLE Your Lynn manages to keep them happy.

MARK It's different for Lynn.

MIRABELLE Because she makes it different.

MARK No! Look, my parents – nice people and all that, right – well, they've always been keen for me to get on, climb the ladder, pass the exam, right?

MIRABELLE Yes. And you should be grateful.

MARK I'm oozing with gratitude.

MIRABELLE Oh, very smart.

MARK Sorry, sorry, sorry. Speaking seriously, I am grateful. Right?

MIRABELLE Yes.

MARK So, full of gratitude, I go away to college, to London, to you...

MIRABELLE Thank you.

MARK All so that my life can have more possibilities, wider horizons or whatever than theirs.

MIRABELLE Yes, precisely.

MARK And having gone through all this, all to be different from them... then they want me to pretend that I'm still the same. And so do you by the sound of it.

MIRABELLE Nobody expects you to be the same...

MARK No! Same beliefs, same values, same outlook? Everything's been done for fifteen years of my education to make me different and now people want to know why I'm different! And I'm supposed to be the one who's awkward!

Mirabelle laughs despite herself.

(*Pause*) So... friends again?

MIRABELLE (*pause*) Friends again.

Mark lets out a long sigh of relief.

It doesn't make for very happy families though, does it?

MARK They'll get over it. Just as we have.

MIRABELLE Oh, I'm sorry I got all uptight about it.

MARK No... I thought you survived it all very well. To say you're a newcomer to the game.

MIRABELLE What makes you think I'm such a newcomer?

MARK I mean to the family punch-up.

MIRABELLE Yes. I have parents too, you know.

MARK Hmm. I must confess I had rather overlooked that point.

MIRABELLE Next holiday we'll go and stay with them.

MARK Yes! It'll be nice to be a spectator for a change.

MIRABELLE Promise you won't threaten to leave me afterwards though.

MARK I promise. Not ever afterwards.

MIRABELLE Then it's a deal.

Producing Radio Plays in Schools

It is often thought that radio plays consist of a lot of sound effects joined together by lines of dialogue. Consequently, beginners often clutter their plays with pops, bangs and background noises in the hope that these will give a play a radio flavour. In fact, a play written for radio depends, like any other form of drama, on a writer creating characters and then causing tensions between them which make the listener want to know what is going to happen next. However technically brilliant a production may be, unless people in the story are convincing and interesting the attention of the audience will soon wander.

The radio producer's job is to mix the voices and sound effects and also to take note of the important silences so that the meaning becomes clear. Sounds in real life are often muddled and confusing: if you doubt that, listen to the actual events at Westminster when the BBC broadcasts Today in Parliament and you might believe that you were listening to a lot of silly sheep rather than intelligent men and women. If you have ever tried to record a conversation at a party you will realise just how difficult it is to capture a lively atmosphere without drowning the dialogue. The producer has to select and balance sounds so that the words stand out clearly, and also make sure that we know just who is present in each scene and who is speaking.

When you listen to radio plays you notice just how important it is to name the characters early on. It is even necessary to alter lines in the great classics to establish who is speaking to whom. This is particularly true with the plays of Shakespeare which usually have so many characters that it becomes difficult for the listener to hold them all in his head. Doors play an essential part in establishing just who is in or out of a room and actors have to make sure that they leave chinks in the dialogue to allow the opening and closing of doors, as characters join or leave a scene, to register with the audience. A modern professional sound studio is crammed full of expensive and sophisticated equipment and the sight can be daunting when you start to consider the possibility of producing a radio play. Before talking about the basic requirements for producing plays in school, it may be useful to know what you would expect to see in a BBC drama studio.

The actors perform in a large room that is divided into several areas which have been specially treated to provide different sound qualities. One section has a hard "live" quality which could be used to indicate that we are in a school assembly hall or a large open-plan office. Another is fitted with a series of screens to represent the acoustic or "sound atmosphere" that you might expect in an ordinary living room, and, tucked away in a corner is a small room, heavily blanketed to absorb sound, to provide the so-called "dead" acoustic which is used to suggest that we are out of doors. Although listeners are not always consciously aware of the different sound quality as the play moves from one scene to another, the acoustic contrasts provide variety and add to the realism of the production. A member of the audio staff works close to the actors, providing all of the practical effects like striking matches or opening and closing doors which the actors, script in hand, would find difficult to do for themselves.

In the control cubicle, which is a self-contained area completely separate from the studio in which the actors perform, sit the producer and production secretary who has the important duty of timing each scene with a stop watch. Programme planning makes exact demands and every play has to fit into an allotted slot. Listeners expect certain programmes at particular times, and if productions were all allowed to over-run there would soon be chaos. The production secretary makes constant checks to see that the actors aren't speeding up or slowing down from one rehearsal to the next. Visitors are often surprised at the importance attached to timing, but it is a discipline that the professional producer soon comes to accept.

With the producer and production secretary there are usually two members of the audio staff. One technician looks after the records and tapes which have to be played in, from a bank of record players and tape decks, to provide background noises – these might include the sound of machinery in a factory, the dawn chorus to suggest an early spring morning, the whoosh of a rocket or extravagant crashes in a comedy sequence. In the centre of the cubicle sits the senior technician, the panel operator, who works a number of volume controls which mix and balance the voices of the actors with the effects which are fed to him from the discs and tapes. The control panel also has special facilities that allow the operator to change the quality of the voices by adding filters to suggest a telephone conversation, echo to give the illusion of a dungeon and a host of other devices. In recent years there have been some moves towards location recordings where the cast go out with the technical staff and record the play in a real setting but because of the problems of weather and "sounds off" – the aeroplane which decides to fly overhead as you are recording a nativity play, for example – location recording is the exception rather than the rule.

If you decide to record some of the plays in this volume, or others that you have written yourself, you will be freed from the restriction of exact timings and although it may take longer to make satisfactory recordings with basic equipment a great deal can be achieved with a little imagination. Remember that much of the expensive machinery used in a professional studio is there to save the time and cost of the actors and technical staff.

In your control room you will need a small mixer-panel so that the producer and technicians can listen to the output and adjust the volume of sounds from the microphone and effects tapes. You will need two tape recorders; one on which to play in effects and the other to record the play so that it can be checked afterwards. A record player is useful as it enables you to play in sound effects which are available commercially. The other essentials are a microphone connected to a loudspeaker in the studio area so that the producer can direct the actors from the control room, and a simple cue light so that he is able to indicate when they should start to speak.

In the acting area you will need to decide what sort of space you wish to convey to the listeners. Even a large echoing space like the school hall can be changed by draping blankets over screens placed around the microphone. If you keep your ears about you, it may be possible to find natural areas which will give contrasts, such as a stone corridor to suggest a gaol or a cupboard to give the "boxy" sound of the cab of a lorry. Excellent results are often gained by simple improvisation. Doors are particularly important and a simple wooden box (it only needs to be about 1.2 metres high) fitted with a variety of locks, doorknobs and latches can suggest a front and back door or, with a suitable chime added, a shop door. A small box fitted with a number of contrasting bells and buzzers is another useful piece of equipment as it enables sounds to be placed where they match the position of the actor who is ringing the doorbell or answering the 'phone.

One of the great advantages of radio is that the actors are not seen. Visitors are often amused when they peep into a BBC studio and discover that the romantic voices that they have just heard in a tender love scene belong to a skinny actor with pebble lens spectacles and a dumpy little actress who has to stand on a box to be the right height for the microphone. This presents the producer with a unique opportunity as it enables actors with flexible voices to play a wide range of parts without being typecast. Your appearance has nothing to do with the person you are able to bring to life through the loudspeaker. A Chinese actor can play a Liverpudlian or a Cockney, a thin man can play a fat man or a plain person become as beautiful as Helen of Troy. Another thing in favour of radio acting is that there is little time in which to get bored! Usually actors are only together for two or three days at a time and may find it refreshing not to have to go through the long process of learning lines by heart. At the same time, good actors usually study the play carefully before coming to the studio. There is a great difference between an intelligent reading of a part at the beginning of rehearsals and the finished performance when the character has developed and found new depths by establishing relationships with the other people in the play.

There are technical tricks of the trade which actors learn with experience, but the basic craft of radio acting is mainly a matter of commonsense. Actors have to move towards or away from the microphone to indicate that they are approaching or leaving; they need to pitch their voices above background sounds to suggest that they are haranguing a crowd or talking over clattering machinery. More importantly, good actors have to develop a creative imagination which enables them to play a love scene or fight their way out from under a pile of rubble whilst actually standing in a large studio holding a script. It is a mistake to feel that the actor has to stand absolutely still when acting to a microphone; in fact, it is almost impossible to act without moving: a close-up of the face of an actor working in a radio studio would show just as much emotion as if he were performing for television.

A word about scripts: obviously they are necessary but the audience must never know they are there. An actor's performance should never sound as if the script is being read and great care has to be taken to turn the pages over quietly as the sound is easily picked up.

Full details of equipment, the operation of tape recorders and recording techniques suitable for schools will be found in the books listed below.

DAVID COLLISON *Stage Sound*, Studio Vista
GRAHAM JONES *Teaching with Tape*, Focal Press
L. MALLORY *The Right Way to Tape Record*, Eliot Right Way Books (easy to use)
KENNETH METHOLD *Broadcasting with Children*, U.L.P.
ALEC NISBETT *The Technique of the Sound Studio*, Focal Press
H. WOODMAN *The Drama Tape Guide*, Focal Press
NATIONAL FOUNDATION FOR VISUAL AIDS *The Tape Recorder in the Classroom* (particularly good on the machine itself)

The control cubicle of a radio drama studio. In the foreground is the senior member of the audio staff who mixes and balances the different sounds. Behind him, on the left, is the producer and next to him, the author. At the back sits the operator who plays in all of the music and effects from tapes and discs.

The producer and writer discussing a problem with members of the cast during a rehearsal of John Arden's play "Pearl". You can see that this end of the drama studio has hard surfaces in order to produce a "live" acoustic. The screens in the background have a soft covering on the reverse side so that they can be used to absorb sound when necessary.

David Calder and Elizabeth Bell recording a radio play. Notice how the actress, even though limited by having to hold a script, uses her hand and facial expression to help produce the emotions she feels.

Writing for Radio

The radio writer's main concern is not with sound effects but with dialogue. He has no scenery, costume or lighting to help in creating an atmosphere and, unlike the novelist, he cannot describe the appearance of his characters except through the words which they address to one another. The dialogue has to do several things simultaneously: it must create character – in a well-written play each person should have a distinctive way of talking and we ought to be able to guess who is speaking without referring to the names printed in the margin; it has to carry the action forward or we will be left with a group of interesting and convincing characters without a story; it must reveal information in a way which appears natural – we have all heard dialogue where the writer elicits information in a clumsy way, like: "Tracy, how long is it since we got married?" or points to something essential to the plot too obviously: "I will put the poison pills, the pink ones, in the blue box." Above all, dialogue must have vitality and spontaneity; conversation which may be passable in real life can sound threadbare and lifeless on radio. Whatever brilliance a director may be able to bring to a script, no amount of embroidery or elaborate sound effect sequences will be able to disguise the fact that a play lacks substance or that an author has not considered his characters in depth.

If you decide to try your hand at writing a play, remember that well-drawn characters and good situations are more important than sound effects, and that a story based on a school trip, a stay in hospital or a clash of personalities in the classroom will probably work out better than a plot about a bank robbery or anything else which you have not experienced at first hand.

The Authors

Chris Curry

Chris Curry was born in Wigan in 1946, the daughter of a coalman. She left school at fifteen with no qualifications apart from 30 words per minute typing. She worked as a typist for a number of firms before marrying at twenty. She started writing five years ago.

Her first radio play, *All We Need is an Elephant*, was broadcast in 1980. It was followed by *Little Weed's Big Day* in 1981, *Mugs' Concert* in 1982 and *Situation Wanted, Save the Whale* and *But Robert Nobody Dies for Love Anymore* in 1983. Her first stage play, *Songs, Wars and People*, written in collaboration with Don Webb, was performed by the Sheffield Vanguard Company in 1982 and she contributed to the Oldham Coliseum's revue, *A Little of What You Fancy*, in the same year.

Gilly Fraser

Gilly Fraser was born in Hunslet, Leeds and went to West Leeds Girls' High School, which she left at sixteen with a few 'O' levels and no very clear ideas about the future except a desire to act.

After drifting about for a couple of years, including a brief spell with Esmé Church's Children's Theatre Company, she was finally turned in the direction of a scholarship to Drama School by a lucky encounter with a sympathetic Youth Employment Officer. She went to the Guildhall School of Music and Drama for two years and then embarked on a career as an actress. This was none too successful and finding herself at thirty with a husband, two children and a long list of credits (but always in small parts) she finally realised that love of drama had more to do with writing it than acting it.

A Quick Visit Home was the first play she ever wrote and was produced in Manchester. She has since written seven plays for radio, the latest being *Somewhere Else* in August 1983. A BBC television Play for Today *Not For The Likes of Us* and many episodes of Angels followed. She has also written for the theatre, most recently *I Can Give You A Good Time* which was written while Writer in Residence at the Royal Court Theatre as the winner of a Thames Television bursary. She has also written two plays for young people – *Blame it on the Boogie* and *Domestic Affair*. She now lives in London.

Wally K. Daly

Wally K. Daly, one of the few English playwrights with a pigtail (one foot long at the time of going to press), was born in the north of England in 1940. Having failed abysmally at school, he left at fifteen to work in the docks for a year, and then tried to save his future by serving an apprenticeship in the local steelworks. During this period he discovered amateur dramatics and soon realised that he wanted to work in the professional theatre. His parents despaired.

Finishing his apprenticeship at twenty-one, he went to London seeking fame, fortune and fun; but most important any sort of occupation connected with entertainment. Since then he has worked as an actor, stage manager, singer, comedian and stage electrician. Fame and fortune aren't quite as important as he once thought they were so he's cancelled them from his list. He became a playwright accidentally in 1974, and hasn't had a proper job since. He lives with his wife Pauline and his two children, Adam 16, and Samantha 11, in a strange turreted house in West London. His best-known work is probably the musical *Follow the Star* of which his children are not very fond.

David Luck

David Luck was born in Watford in 1941, educated at Watford Grammar School (successes include Lent Term 1956: Scripture 7th equal; Summer Term 1957: under 16's 100 yards dash

3rd). He left in 1958 to become a quantity surveyor, working in London and Watford. Following his marriage in 1966 he went to live "North of Watford" and settled in Leeds where he has remained, working for the City Council, for some years in the City Architect's Department before becoming an assistant in the Inner City Office.

In 1979 he joined a creative writing class and in 1981 contributed to BBC Radio 4's anthology Pen to Paper and had one Morning Story broadcast. Two radio plays followed: *Voice Downstairs, Ears Upstairs* (1982) and *An Avalanche of Cows* (1983). His first radio play drew on his experiences as an Adult Literacy Tutor.

Peter Whalley

Peter Whalley was born in Colne, Lancashire in 1946. Twenty-one years later he found himself a schoolteacher in London. Having got married, he applied for a teaching post in Pontefract, West Yorkshire and thus returned northwards in 1971. It was while in Pontefract, and mainly through the stimulus of an amateur dramatic society, that he began to write, initially in his spare-time and then, from 1978, full-time. He has since moved back over the Pennines to Lancaster.

The main incentive for abandoning teaching was an invitation to join the team of writers working on Coronation Street, for which he has now written over forty episodes. Other television work has included episodes of Jury and Angels, a Schools Television series About Books, and two plays – *A Man of Morality* and *Risking It.*

However, for a long time he regarded himself primarily as a radio writer and has written a total of 25 plays for BBC Radio 4, as well as co-writing two drama series – *Cromwell Mansion* and *Top Twenty* – for Piccadilly Radio, Manchester's independent station.

More recently, he has started to write novels. His first two – *Post Mortem* and *The Mortician's Birthday Party*, which are both thrillers – have been published by Macmillan.

Useful Books

Writing for the BBC BBC Publications, 35 Marylebone High Street, London W1
New Radio Drama BBC Publications
GILES COOPER, *Six Plays for Radio*, BBC Publications
HENRY REED, *Radio Plays*, BBC Publications
DON HAWORTH, *Radio Plays*, BBC Publications
Worth a Hearing: Five Radio Plays, Blackie and Son
New English Dramatists Volume 12, Penguin
DONALD MCWHINNIE, *The Art of Radio*, Faber
Out of the Air, Longman (Imprint Books)
IAN RODGER, *Radio Drama*, Macmillan
The Best Radio Plays of 1978/1979/1980/1981/1982, Methuen
JOHN ARDEN, *Pearl, A Radio Play*, Methuen

Questions for Discussion and Suggestions for Writing

A Quick Visit Home

1 Although it's only a device to bring the sisters together, consider first of all the funeral scene. Is it a realistic presentation of such an occasion? What do you think about Pat's remark that she'd rather her father had "had nothing than that gabbled farce"?

2 We learn a good deal about the three women in the family – as they do about each other. Will these discussions have improved their relationship? Can you understand why the mother was ambitious for Lynne? Do you think she was unfair to Pat? To what extent should a parent direct his/her children?

3 Compare the lives led by Lynne and Pat. Why is neither of them satisfied with her "lot"? (Is "lot" in fact the right term here?) If you were producing this play, what kind of voices would you choose for the two sisters?

4 Take Pat first: Jim says to her, "You martyr yourself because you enjoy it." Do you agree – and what do you think of his proposal that she should get a job? What does Pat resent most about Lynne?

5 Now Lynne: Her mother complains, "You don't know what you want." What advice would *you* give Lynne?

6 This play was first transmitted in the mid-nineteen seventies. Does it still reflect the position of women today?

Voice Downstairs, Ears Upstairs

1 Peter says of his son: "Disabled? He's as sound in wind and limb as you are. Or will be. He's not the brightest person I've met." In what way is Andrew disabled? If you were producing this play, would you ask the actor playing Andrew to talk in any particular way?

2 Look carefully at the conversations Jill has with Mrs Verse. Why do you think the playwright added these scenes?
3 What impressions do you get of the family? How is this effect achieved? And what do you feel about each of them?
4 Which of Andrew's "adventures" do you find the most amusing? Which do you think most exasperated Peter? Where else do we find entertainment in this play? Is the play's only purpose to make us laugh?
5 Take any one of the mishaps that Peter reports to Jill and rewrite it as it would be presented in a novel. What does this style of storytelling gain or lose in comparison?
6 Read through some reviews of radio drama you find in daily and Sunday newspapers. Then write a short review of this play.

It's A Wise Child

1 A play like this one reveals just how carefully and quickly a radio playwright creates his or her characters. We can even imagine what Eddie looks like after the first few scenes. See if you can find the key speeches which give the information we need to have about Eddie before the play can develop.
2 We are told that the Grangebank Boys' Club is the winner of the "Northern Area Finals" in the national club drama group competition. What are the other clues that give you the impression that the play is set in a community in the North of England? What do you think of Madelaine's comment about London: "I haven't seen anyone outside our lot smile since we got here"?
3 Is there such a thing as "Northern Humour"? Compare Guv's bantering to Collie's in *Little Weed's Big Day*.
4 When Norm tells Kev what he said to his mum – " 'Hey, I reckon if we knew who Little Eddie's real mam and dad were, we'd know why he was so daft' ", he reports: ". . . she went mad. Really tore into me. 'You leave well alone', she said." Why do you think she was so angry? How do you feel about adopted children looking for their natural parents?
5 When the Guv asks Vi why she hasn't told Eddie the truth, she replies, "I've got a nice husband and two nice kids, Guv. How do you tell a husband you had a baby when you were

sixteen that he knows nowt about?" What would you do in Vi's situation?

6 Eddie's main reason for looking for his real parents is: "If you don't know who they are . . . how can you know when they die?" What do you think of the solution the playwright gives to Eddie's problem? Why is the title of the play so witty?

7 Imagine you are the technician for this play. Write a list of the sound effects you would have to record and suggest how you would produce them. If possible, try to record some.

Little Weed's Big Day

1 "He looks more like that there Little Weed to me," Cheyenne says of Ben after chanting the song of the Flower Pot Men. See if you can work out how all the other nicknames came to be given to the coalmen.

2 Would you like to work for Jem? Do you think he should have let Ben take the dog home? Why is Collie so likeable? Does it surprise you he stands by and watches Ben trying to lift the hammer?

3 At the end of the day Collie tries to explain to Ben: "Look lad, there's things you don't know . . . " What incidents during the day have revealed Ben's innocence?

4 How could the actor playing Jem convey his changes of mood during the course of the play?

5 Script and record the conversation Ben and his mother have that evening.

6 If you have a "Saturday job" or had any part-time employment, try and remember what happened and how you felt on your first day. A group of you could pool your experiences and produce a play from them.

Home Truths

1 "Bringing the girl/boyfriend home" for the first time is an occasion most of us dread. Why should this be so, and why do we, like Mark, waste breath in advance, trying to apologise for our parents? What impression does Mark try to give Mirabelle of his home life, and how does his family behave

in reality? Ask a friend who knows your family well to write a description of them, and discuss what you learn from such a viewpoint.

2 Both Mark and his parents are obviously relieved that the visit – until the last twenty-four hours anyway – is so relaxed and good-tempered. Mark says of his parents: "They do seem to have improved a bit", while Lynn informs Mirabelle that she's "changed our Mark". To what do *you* attribute the warm atmosphere in the household?

3 Father Drabble's arrival certainly disturbs the peace. What sort of a person is the priest, and what does he expect to do on this particular afternoon? Does he in fact achieve anything? (You might like to look carefully at the discussion on pages 156–158 before you answer.)

4 One of the key remarks that the playwright makes in talking about images of God and belief in God, is "it's all a question of environment". This leads Mark to ask: "If I'm an atheist only because of my background, are you a priest only because of yours?" What do you think of this idea? Do you regret that your parents have given you the religious or non-religious upbringing that you have received? What role do you think parents should or can play in terms of a religious belief?

5 At the end of the afternoon, Father Drabble comments to Mark, "The real pity is that before your mother arrived you were just beginning to show how religious you really are." How has this shown itself? What is your notion of "being religious"?

6 In what ways does the "discussion" unsettle Mrs Baldwin? Mark too is upset, and unable to call a truce. How would an actor show this when he speaks such lines as "I simply said that I wouldn't mind a fried tomato" at breakfast on the next day? What would your explanation be to Lynn if she asked what had caused the angry atmosphere? What has Mirabelle learnt about Mark as a result of the priest's visit?

7 Mark's final point about his family is that "Everything's been done for fifteen years of my education to make me different and now people want to know why I'm different! And I'm supposed to be the one who's awkward!" To what extent do you think that this is the basis of any "generation gap"? What can children and parents do to ease such a situation? How does a generation gap reveal itself in your

family? You might like to recall an incident and to write (and record) a script on this topic.

General Questions

These questions would best be considered after a careful reading of the page on "Writing for Radio".

1 The opening of any play is always important. Why is this particularly so of radio plays? Choose two opening scenes from the plays in this book, and discuss why each forms a suitable introduction to the events that follow and to our understanding of the characters.

2 "Unlike the novelist, the radio writer cannot describe the appearance of his characters except through the words they address to one another." Choose any two characters from the plays, and describe how you visualise their physical appearance. What clues did you use to arrive at that particular picture in your imagination?

3 "In a well-written play each person should have a distinctive way of talking."
Take one of the plays and cast it from your class, discussing the best use of voices. To what extent are you influenced by a similarity in personality to the character being portrayed? Is this fair? Must many of your actors adopt new voices?

4 "The dialogue has to do several things simultaneously: it must create character . . . it has to carry the action forward . . . it must reveal information in a way which appears natural . . . Above all dialogue must have vitality and spontaneity." Choose one scene from any of the plays which seems to you to achieve all the aims mentioned in this passage. Look at it in detail and explain carefully why you have chosen that particular scene.

5 "The radio writer has no scenery, costume or lighting to help in creating an atmosphere."
What would you gain, and what would you lose, by transferring these plays to the stage, or to television? Choose one play on which to focus your views.

Longman Imprint Books
General Editor: Michael Marland CBE

Titles in the series:

There is a Happy Land Keith Waterhouse
Nine African Stories Doris Lessing
The Experience of Colour *edited by* Michael Marland
***The Human Element and other stories** Stan Barstow
***The Leaping Lad and other stories** Sid Chaplin
Z Cars Four television scripts
Conflicting Generations Five television scripts
***A Sillitoe Selection** *edited by* Michael Marland
***Late Night on Watling Street and other stories** Bill Naughton
Black Boy Richard Wright
The Millstone Margaret Drabble
Fair Stood the Wind for France H.E. Bates
Scene Scripts Seven television plays
The Experience of Work *edited by* Michael Marland
Breaking Away *edited by* Marilyn Davies *and* Michael Marland
The Kraken Wakes John Wyndham
A Hemingway Selection *edited by* Dennis Pepper
Friends and Families *edited by* Eileen *and* Michael Marland
Ten Western Stories *edited by* C.E.J. Smith
The Good Corn and other stories H.E. Bates
The Experience of Sport *edited by* John L. Foster
Loves, Hopes and Fears *edited by* Michael Marland
A Casual Acquaintance and other stories Stan Barstow
Eight American Stories *edited by* D.L. James
Cider with Rosie Laurie Lee
The L-Shaped Room Lynne Reid Banks
The Pressures of Life Four television plays
The Experience of Prison *edited by* David Ball
Saturday Night and Sunday Morning Alan Sillitoe
A John Wain Selection *edited by* Geoffrey Halson
Goalkeepers are Crazy Brian Glanville
A James Joyce Selection *edited by* Richard Adams
Out of the Air Five radio plays, *edited by* Alfred Bradley
Could It Be? *edited by* Michael Marland
The Minority Experience *edited by* Michael Marland *and* Sarah Ray
Scene Scripts Two Five television plays
Caribbean Stories *edited by* Michael Marland
An Isherwood Selection *edited by* Geoffrey Halson
A Thomas Hardy Selection *edited by* Geoffrey Halson
While They Fought *edited by* Michael Marland *and* Robin Willcox
The Wave and other stories Liam O'Flaherty
Irish Short Stories *edited by* Frances Crowe
The Experience of Parenthood *edited by* Chris Buckton
The Experience of Love *edited by* Michael Marland
Twelve War Stories *edited by* John L. Foster
The Birds and other stories Daphne du Maurier
A Roald Dahl Selection *edited by* Roy Blatchford
A D.H. Lawrence Selection *edited by* Geoffrey Halson
I'm the King of the Castle Susan Hill
Sliding Leslie Norris
Scene Scripts Three Four television plays

* Cassette available

Still Waters and other plays *edited by* Alison Leake
Juliet Bravo Five television scripts, *edited by* Alison Leake
Television Comedy Scripts Five television scripts, *edited by* Roy Blatchford
Meetings and Partings *edited by* Michael Marland
A Laurie Lee Selection *edited by* Chris Buckton
Strange Meeting Susan Hill
Looks and Smiles Barry Hines
Family Circles *edited by* Alfred Bradley and Alison Leake
Humour and Horror Five plays *edited by* Caroline Bennitt
P'tang, Yang Kipperbang and other TV plays by Jack Rosenthal